MW01227032

A LIFE RICH WITH
significance

Transforming Your Wealth
to Meaningful Impact

A LIFE RICH WITH

significance

Transforming Your Wealth
to Meaningful Impact

SANGER D. SMITH

BFA™, APMA®, CEPA™

NICHE PRESSWORKS

A Life Rich with Significance

ISBN-13: Paperback 978-1-952654-76-3
          eBook 978-1-952654-77-0

Copyright © 2023 by SANGER SMITH

All rights reserved. No part of this book may be used or reproduced in any manner whatsoever without prior written consent of the author, except as provided by the United States of America copyright law.

Please note that the information presented in this book is for general informational purposes only and should not be construed as legal or financial advice. The content of this book is not intended to create, and receipt of it does not constitute, a lawyer-client nor financial advisor-client relationship. The author, publisher, and any other affiliated parties are not responsible for any actions taken or not taken based on the information provided in this book. Before making any financial or legal decisions, it is recommended that you consult with a qualified professional who can provide personalized advice tailored to your specific situation.

Scripture quotations are taken from The Authorized (King James) Version. Reproduced under public domain.

For permission to reprint portions of this content or for bulk purchases, email contact@decidedlywealth.com.

Published by Niche Pressworks: http://NichePressworks.com
Indianapolis, IN
The views expressed herein are solely those of the author and do not necessarily reflect the views of the publisher.

Dedication

To Mark, Meg, Troy, Jeff, Toni, Sally, Gary, Tina, and Shawn —
knowing you is what provided the inspiration for my work.

About the *Book*

You don't need to wait until your golden years to enjoy the fruits of your labor. Further, getting to your golden years isn't the aim of life. Quitting your job is not the reason you ought to save money.

The financial planning and advice industry prides itself on presenting you with prepackaged, cookie-cutter solutions. We all recognize this inconvenient truth. What goes unnoticed by most is that the problems they identify in your life seem to be the same for your neighbors, friends, and family, too. We're entering a new age — no longer is the highest aim for your money to give you the ability to quit your job at 65 and sit in a rocking chair for the next thirty years. But that's what the industry offers — to help you retire and "meet your goals," whatever that means. What happens when you don't know what your goals are? How do you live a meaningful life before retirement? How can your money do more than simply provide a modest income stream in your sixties and seventies?

A Life Rich with Significance answers these deep questions and explores the mindset of people who find meaning and impact with their wealth before, during, and after their peak earning years.

What does meaningful impact look like for you and your family? If you can find the answer to that question, the other pieces fall into place. This book will help you do that.

Contents

CHAPTER 1

The Real Advice You *Need*

"Aim at the highest possible good that you can conceive of. Having aligned yourself with that good, speak the truth and see what happens. That's the act of faith as whatever the truth reveals is the best of both possible worlds regardless of what it appears to you now." — Dr. Jordan B. Peterson

Once upon a time, it was easy to know whom to trust. We humans lived in small villages, in cabins next door to our parents, in-laws, siblings, and friends. We built communities based on trust. When we needed advice, we knew who to go to. We knew the strengths of each member of our tribe. Each generation passed down its ancestral knowledge, and the greatest keepers of wisdom earned the marker of gray hair and wrinkled skin. In an age where survival was a daily chore, we respected the elderly simply because they had conquered the remarkable feat of staying alive for so long. Early man could seek almost any advice he needed by merely asking the oldest member of his tribe. The elders had seen it all. Before we had the metaverse, smart homes, and artificial intelligence to give us all the answers, the tribal elders were the sole source of knowledge on all matters of importance. "Is this suspiciously delicious plant safe to eat?" Better ask the older generation; they've probably seen someone try it before.

Seeking advice was easy, and accepting it was even easier. With less information, we did not have the luxury of getting a second opinion. Better yet, we rarely fell victim to confirmation bias — unconsciously seeking information aligned with our preconceived notions. We didn't have the option. Now, in the Internet Age, one in five Americans suffers from information overload. This causes brain fog, which stifles the decision-making process.[1]

To grasp the amount of information constantly available to you, consider the palm-sized device in your pocket right now. In 2020, the internet held sixty-four zettabytes of data.[2] A zettabyte is one trillion gigabytes. In 2023, the largest iPhone could store 512 gigabytes of data. That means the internet has more information than 125 billion of the highest data storage iPhones. If every man, woman, and child on this earth had seventeen iPhones and downloaded unique data from the internet onto their device, there would still be dark corners of the web left undiscovered.

So, what do you do when you want advice? Turning to the internet will leave you overloaded with too much information, much of it either incorrect or not applicable to your specific problem. What if, worse yet, you are entirely wrong about what your problem is? The reality, I've learned, is that this is the dilemma we as Americans face in getting money advice. An abundance of information is available, yet most of it is objectively terrible. Even worse, most people seek solutions for the wrong problems entirely — so not only are they getting the wrong answer, but they're also trying to solve the wrong problem in the first place.

WHY FOCUSING ON GOALS IS THE WRONG APPROACH

As the managing partner of a private wealth firm with over $1 billion in assets under advisement, I recognized the extent of how crippling this decision paralysis can be. Yet, I neither faulted my clients nor the average American retail investor. The industry markets to you daily, telling you, "Save to meet your goals." They run expensive ad campaigns highlighting how their unique process, service, website, and mobile app will help you meet your goals better than all the others.

As a financial advisor, I spent years proudly telling clients and potential clients that I "help people make great money decisions so they can meet their goals."

Now, be honest with yourself. Do you really have financial goals? Alternatively, did you have financial goals before you met your financial advisor? If you did, good for you. You're ahead of most people. Now ask yourself why you have those goals. What is the reason for saying you want to retire at 55, buy a beach house, or send your kids to college? Goals are markers along the long, arduous trail of success. What are you aiming at?

FINDING SIGNIFICANCE AFTER DEATH

If you're like my client Oliver, you probably don't know how to answer that. Oliver and I first started working together several years ago. Our relationship began when his wife, Charlotte, died of cancer. Charlotte and I had worked together on the traditional building blocks of a financial plan. She, the high earner of the family, had saved plenty of money by age 55 so that she and Oliver could retire whenever they chose. She and Oliver had amassed enough money in qualified education savings plans to send their daughters to any private university in the country for four years. They had paid off their house years ago. They had no debt. Lastly, she made sure to have solid life insurance if the worst were to happen. When the worst did happen, Oliver instantly became even wealthier than he thought he ever would. Everything true about his financial life during Charlotte's life was now doubly true. On paper, there was no reason for Oliver to have a single concern about money. Yet he did.

About a week after Charlotte passed, Oliver drove from New Mexico to visit me in my Fort Worth, Texas, office to discuss their accounts. That's quite a drive for a conversation that could easily happen over the phone or via video call. When he walked through the door that day, it was the first time I had seen his face. Charlotte and I had always worked together over video chats, and since the family lived nine hours away by car, we never met in person. Moreover, Oliver was simply uninterested in money conversations. He knew Charlotte was incredibly bright, disciplined, and worthy of his trust when making important financial decisions for their family. Whenever Charlotte and I talked, Oliver left us to our business while he stayed in the garage fixing up old cars.

In person, Oliver was exactly what I expected. He dressed like a man who spends his weekends working on the old Mustang he picked up for cheap at the local junkyard. He wore stained denim shorts, rugged work boots, and a T-shirt with the American flag on it.

Before he could even sit down on the sofa, he said, "I know we could've done this over the phone, but this all stresses me out, so I would rather be here in person."

"I can't imagine how difficult it must be to lose your wife," I said, attempting to be empathetic.

"Yeah, of course, I'm sad about that. That isn't what stresses me out, though. I'm worried I'm going to run out of money."

"Well, then, I have great news. Based on what you spend, you could put every single dollar you own in cash, never earn a penny of interest, and your children will still never run out of money."

Oliver and I repeated different versions of this same conversation every three months for the next two years. He would drive his truck for a whole day across state lines to my office to tell me he feared he'd run out of money, and I'd show him all the charts and graphs that said otherwise. He'd go sleep in his hotel room, drive back home to New Mexico the next morning, and then we would repeat it all over again about ninety days later.

Yet, no matter what, Oliver never stopped being more frugal with his spending than you can imagine. He didn't need to work, but he continued to work a job he complained about daily because he didn't believe he could afford to quit. Often, between our quarterly meetings, we would have phone calls with the same theme. Oliver would call me out of the blue and say, "Hey, Sanger, I saw the market was down; is everything going to be alright?"

"Yes, Oliver. Like I've said before, you could quit your job, pull half your money out of your accounts, light it on fire, and you still won't run out of money."

The more we had this same conversation, the more I questioned my own skills as an advisor. I would think to myself, "Am I failing at my job? How does he not see that he shouldn't worry about running out of money? Maybe the illustrations I'm putting together aren't as good as I think."

After nearly two years into our relationship, Oliver had yet to make a single withdrawal from his account. So, it became a perverse goal of my own to get Oliver to spend his money. Unfortunately, what I was doing wasn't working, so I changed my tactics. Instead of simply showing Oliver that he wouldn't run out of money, I started to brainstorm with him on ways to spend his money. "He loves cars," I thought. "Maybe he could buy a new car instead of driving that raggedy old truck. Yes! That's a great idea, especially since he drives nearly halfway across the country four times a year as it is."

"Hey, Oliver, how about treating yourself to a new truck?"

"No, I don't need to spend money on something like that."

So, I thought harder. He seems keen on finding a reason to leave New Mexico, so what about a second home somewhere he'll enjoy being? So, the next time Oliver called, I presented my latest idea. "What do you think about buying a cabin in Colorado?" I asked. "You love the mountains there! Heck, you could even buy a house in Fort Worth, too, since you come here so often. It could be your getaway from the same tired, one-stoplight town when you want it."

"No, I don't have that kind of money."

A conversation with Oliver about his daughters' college savings accounts forever changed my philosophy regarding how to help my clients tackle the problems that truly matter. I had gone to Austin for my old college roommate's wedding and was starting the three-hour drive back home to Fort Worth, jamming out to Willie Nelson alone in my truck, when my ringtone interrupted my horrendous singing. I looked down and saw Oliver's name on the caller ID. It was a Saturday. Usually, clients, even Oliver, don't call on the weekend. I figured he desperately needed to talk, so I picked up immediately.

"Hey, Oliver! I didn't expect to hear from you today. How's your weekend?"

"Yeah, it's uh... it's fine — it's — it's — it's... not fine, actually. I'm pissed off." Before I could ask what was wrong, he quickly went on, "How much money is in the college savings accounts? You're always saying I won't run out of money, so can I just give it all away? Will I run out of money if I give it all away, or do I need to keep it?"

The nature of the question didn't allow me to celebrate that this was the first time Oliver had acknowledged he had more money than he needed to sustain his lifestyle. This wasn't the first time he was upset with his daughters, but it was the first time he let it influence his decisions with his money. The girls had been having a tough time after losing their mother — that's understandable. Imagine being a single dad raising two teenage daughters in a tiny town with no extended family nearby. All three of them were hurting.

Of course, any decent father suffers unimaginable pain when his relationship with his children is fractured. Yet, when I reflected on what I knew about Oliver, I realized more about why he was in such a deep depression. When we started working together, we discussed his values — what mattered most to him. He mentioned many things during that conversation — his faith, a love of the outdoors, and security. But, most of all, he mentioned relationships. His entire life, Oliver had dedicated resources, time, and energy to nurturing the relationships most important to him. When the relationship with Charlotte — the most important relationship he had ever experienced — ended upon her death, he suffered terribly. And now, instead of having his daughters to turn to, he suffered in his relationship with them, too.

Yet, he didn't have to continue that unhappy situation. Oliver's question made me realize his wealth could do something meaningful for him. With creative thinking, he could begin to repair that damaged relationship with his daughters. Not only that, but he could also finally express his real values so others would know him better.

Oliver is a man who desperately wants to be seen, even though he spends his life away from the hustle and bustle of big cities, large concerts, and the like. He will rarely appear in a crowd of more than five people, but you better believe those four other people will know the love he has for others. He is frugal with money but even more frugal with the time and commitment he spends on others. When he does spend that energy, he goes all out.

In an episode of my podcast, I had the privilege of hosting my friend Buddy Wakefield, one of the most significant modern American poets. He shared with me, "Being witnessed is fundamental to the infrastructure of healing." To be witnessed in the sense Buddy spoke about is to be seen and edified for who you are at your core. Oliver was not doing this for his daughters, and they were not doing it for him. And at this moment, Oliver was desperately begging for someone to witness him, whether or not he recognized it.

"Oliver," I said calmly, "If there was something you could do to have a better relationship with your daughters, would you do it?"

"Yeah, of course, but there's nothing I can do."

"When was the last time you spent time together, just the three of you?"

"Well, I don't know... after the funeral, maybe. They don't want anything to do with me; they just want to do their own thing."

"How about this?" I suggested. "Why don't you use your money to make that time together happen?"

Oliver and I planned a trip of a lifetime for him and his daughters. We specifically designed the trip to allow each of them to witness and be witnessed by each other. First, they went to Europe together and saw all the sights the girls dreamed of seeing — the Eiffel tower in Paris and Big Ben in London. Then they went hiking, an activity Oliver loves when they're back home in New Mexico. Only this time, they did it in Scotland. This wasn't simply a vacation — it was an experience designed for each member of the family to show the others something important to them and share in the joy of that together.

The trip brought the family together in a way they had not experienced since their Charlotte had passed. Now, for Oliver and his daughters, the once-in-a-lifetime experience has become an annual tradition.

Knowing that his money will outlive him, Oliver spends time on these trips discussing his daughters' future inheritance with them. He explains how he wants that money to deepen their own relationships with their children one day. He uses the opportunity created by those moments to transfer his values to them so his and Charlotte's legacy can live on past their time on Earth.

THE HIGHEST AIM FOR YOUR MONEY

With this book, I want to change the way you think about money so you may transform wealth to significance. The tools exist within you; I'll show you how to find them. The problem with advice today is that it begins with solutions instead of first seeking the truest problem we could solve. Solutions should never start with product-based advice. Charlatans present ready-made solutions seeking an audience. The right type of advice is not tax advice, debt reduction, or even goal achievement. The right advice is first to decide who you are. What is the core importance of your money? What do you want your money to do? What is the purpose of all this?

As an American in the twenty-first century with enough money to even consider speaking with a financial advisor, you are one of the very wealthiest people to have ever lived. You might not like acknowledging that reality, but it is the truth. You, reading this right now, are wealthier than 99 percent of the people who have ever walked this earth.

Most of the advice in the marketplace is tactical. It's not for you. At the very least, it's not for you... yet. You do not know whether the tactical advice you watch on YouTube is the advice you should take unless you have first decided who you are. And you have not decided who you are unless you have first decided upon your highest and best aim.

PROVERBS 12:15

CHAPTER 2

The Consequences
of *Aiming Low*

*"Alexander the Great and his mule driver both died.
The same thing happened to both." – Marcus Aurelius*

It is not obvious that your money can, or even should, mean anything approaching significance. Our consumerist society inundates us with new ways to spend our money on "stuff." When pundits elaborate on the success of capitalism or the global reduction of poverty, they often cite figures such as how many people now have televisions in their homes or smartphones in their pockets. In a culture where people know the most-watched annual sporting event as much for its commercial advertisements as for the football game being played, who can blame anyone for seeing material possessions as objective, broad indicators of lifestyle improvement and success?

I do know, though, what it looks like when money means nothing to someone — when it does not bring significance.

As the son of an investment advisor, I started working for my father's business when I was fourteen. All I knew at that time was that the family business "helped rich people stay rich," as my father would put it when he was being coy about his profession at dinner parties. But a death in the family and a dusty hunting rifle made me realize what we were really bringing to the families for whom we worked — because I saw what it looked like when someone didn't have it.

FINDING MEANING WITH A HUNTING RIFLE

Roger Shelton was my grandfather, but from the time I learned to speak, I followed suit with the rest of the family and called him Ogie. Ogie was born in the small West Texas town of Pecos. Like most men from the Rural West, he wore pearl-snap shirts and cowboy boots every day. He had a large, bushy mustache that looked like Tom Selleck's would if he perpetually misplaced his comb. Ogie loved riding horses, hunting deer, listening to Willie Nelson, and smoking cigarettes. It's the cigarettes that did him in.

During my entire childhood, Ogie was in and out of the hospital. Visiting my grandpa was rarely a celebration but rather a cautious call of duty because we never knew if the next visit would come. For the last ten years of his life, we rarely visited Ogie outside a sterile hospital room. Instead, my mother would gather my two sisters and me in the kitchen and tell us, "Today, we're driving out to see your grandpa. Y'all need to go because this might be the last time." On a rainy April day during my senior year of high school, it was the last time. He passed peacefully in his bed in his own house, surrounded by family.

As my family and I were leaving his home that evening after he passed, his wife stopped me before I got out the door. She was not my biological grandmother; she had married my grandfather decades before I, his oldest grandchild, was even born. "Please come back tomorrow. I have some of Ogie's things I want to give you," she told me.

The next day, I drove out to the humble town where he had spent the last several years of his life. At his house, Ogie's wife showed me her coffee table, on which lay a couple of his maroon pearl-snap shirts and his old Remington .25-06 hunting rifle in a yellow leather case. I thanked her for the gifts, drove home, and didn't think about it much again.

During deer season seven months later, I walked through a field on my family's ranch near Hico, Texas, with Ogie's old hunting rifle draped over my shoulder. I had set out that morning before the sun even thought of rising, hoping to honor my grandfather's memory by using his old rifle as he would have liked to if not for the pesky hospital visits in his way. Trying not to make a single sound, I tiptoed through the field carefully, ensuring not to step on a twig or rustle too many leaves. I could barely see twelve inches in front of me. Unfortunately, the rain clouds shielded the moon's light from its attempt to aid me.

Suddenly, I stopped dead in my tracks as, out of nowhere, I sensed danger. I inhaled a slow, deep breath through my nostrils to confirm my initial fear: Something was burning. A brush fire would ruin this morning's hunt and my family's land. I was now dripping with anxiety. I looked over to my left. A trickle of light peered over the horizon and faintly illuminated the treetops. Yet still, I saw no smoke. I stood on my tiptoes, lifted my chin, and squinted my eyes, staring straight ahead through the hay field — still no sign of fire. Finally, I turned my head to the right and, this time, sharply sucked air in through my nose. That's when it hit me.

There was no brush fire. What I smelled was the leather strap of Ogie's old rifle that had not remembered to let go of the smell of his cigarette smoke. I laughed, thinking, "There's no chance of sneaking up on a twelve-point buck smelling like Marlboro Smooths." So, I lumbered back to my truck, placed the rifle under the back seat, hopped in the front, and took off down the dirt road.

Wanting to make the most of this moment of connection with my grandfather, I turned the speakers to play "Uncloudy Day" by Willie Nelson. It was one of the songs he insisted we play at his funeral. When I pulled my truck to the end of the dirt road onto the main highway, I didn't turn left to go home. Instead, I turned right, toward the cemetery.

When I pulled in through the gates, I drove to where I remembered his gravesite to be — right next to his brother and his parents. When I got out of the truck and walked over, all that I saw was a soft pile of dirt. There was not even a headstone.

Inconsolable rage fired within me at the disrespect to Ogie, and I immediately called my mom and berated her far more sternly than any young man should ever speak to his mother. "Why does your own father not have a headstone?"

To my confusion, she responded calmly, without even a hint of shock at the idea of her father resting in an unmarked grave. Instead of the response I expected, she replied in only a mildly annoyed tone, "I paid for his funeral. Someone else can pay for the headstone."

At that moment, I knew that the old Remington hunting rifle was the only thing my grandfather had left when he died.

He didn't have enough money for a funeral. He didn't even have enough money for a headstone.

I later learned that, despite flirting with death for a decade, my grandfather died intestate. He died without even bothering to complete a will. Not only did he not leave any*thing* behind, but he also denied himself the opportunity to pass along his values. He neglected his obligation to create a legacy of significance. Instead, his legacy became one of debt, destitution, and financial burden for his wife and children, who had to spend their own money to mourn his loss to create some semblance of a legacy for him.

DEATH COMES FOR US ALL

Roman Emperor Marcus Aurelius wisely said, "Alexander the Great and his mule driver both died, and the same thing happened to both."

Alexander the Great was one of the most outstanding military leaders in history, known for his campaigns and conquests across Asia and Europe. He had a vast army of soldiers at his disposal, but he also had a trusted advisor in the form of a simple mule driver. Despite their differences in status and power, death was the ultimate equalizer. Whether you are a prominent leader or a mule driver, death will come for you no matter who you are. In the grand scheme of things, the distinctions and differences between us all are insignificant compared to the inevitability of death.

We will all end up in the ground, y'all. So, there's no choice but to live life with purpose and humility, aimed toward the highest good we can conceive.

LEGACY IS NOT MONEY ALONE

Transforming wealth to significance does not mean leaving a hefty sum of money behind for your kids to spend once you are gone. No, it means to orient your wealth to achieve its greatest impact during your life — with a velocity so powerful and an aim so high that the momentum of your pursuit of good continues generationally.

Monetary goal achievement alone is unfulfilling. Successfully achieving goals does not indicate ultimate success. Rather, goals are trail markers along the journey toward success. Setting and achieving goals is not an aim itself but a tool to measure your progress toward your highest aim. Author Kathy Kolbe defines success as "the freedom to be yourself." A goal may measure one's progress toward this aim. The main traditional financial goal of retirement clearly illustrates this. If your job prevents you from being yourself, retiring from that job and instead orienting your time and energy toward the activities that allow you to be true to who you are would be an indicator of success. However, simply saving and investing such that you can quit your job is not success. Retirement in and of itself is not success. Rather, it is akin to a mile marker along the highway of success. And the sad truth is that even the clear and focused pursuit of this traditional idea of success is often not satisfying.

SUCCESS IS UNFULFILLING

The reason this traditional notion of success is ultimately unfulfilling is that it focuses inward. Even the most eloquent interpretation of success as a concept, like Kolbe's definition, is ultimately self-focused.

On the other hand, significance (in the context of this book) focuses outward. Much like John F. Kennedy's call to Americans, "Ask not what your country can do for you; ask what you can do for your country," we should invert our thinking regarding our wealth. Instead of thinking, "How can I achieve my goals and my success and my aims?", we should say, "How can this wealth I am blessed to steward make this world a better place for others?" If you focus your efforts externally and orient the purpose of your wealth to others — your children, your spouse, your community, your country — you cannot help but attain significance. In that event, success will be a consequential by-product of a much more noble cause.

Christ said in Matthew 23:12, "And whosoever shall exalt himself shall be abased; and he that shall humble himself shall be exalted." Goals for the sake of goals, and success more broadly, are an exercise in the exaltation of the self. A humbled self can view wealth as a tool to provide more to the world rather than simply to obtain more material possessions.

THE PHONE CALL THAT CHANGED MY LIFE

"Ring... Ring... RING... RING!'"

As a pulse of cortisol rushed through my veins, I opened my eyes wide enough to see the tiny red light flashing on the telephone.

I stood up quickly from the couch and shuffled over to the desk with my right hand outstretched to make sure I didn't bang my knees against the granite table. "Hello, this is Sanger. How may I help you?"

Stunned silence ensued for a moment. Then a voice replied, "Uh... um — I assumed I'd be getting your voicemail."

I stared out the large window of my fourth-floor office. There wasn't a car in sight. "May I ask who's calling?"

"It's John. Why the heck are you coming into the office at four in the morning?"

I wasn't at the office at four in the morning because I got an early start to my day. I was at the office at four in the morning because I never went home. "Work hard, play hard. Right, John?"

Now, it was my turn to be stunned as he replied.

"Look, Sanger, I'm counting on you to manage my family's wealth." He saw right through my façade. "I need you to be okay, and working till 4:00 a.m. isn't okay."

Frankly, I don't remember what I said to John after that. What I do remember is the hopeless feeling of knowing that he was right. Working my fingers to the bone past midnight, falling asleep on the couch in my office, waking up before sunrise, bathing myself in the office sink, then chugging three cups of coffee to maintain composure before my employees arrived each morning was not a long-term recipe for success. I knew the truth as soon as John hit me with a dose of reality. Living like this would kill me. It was a disservice to me, my employees, and my clients.

For six months, that wretched morning routine had become an all-too-common occurrence. When I was twenty-four, I bought the company my father founded. We hadn't ever discussed the significance of this business to him. We hadn't ever talked about how to make big decisions involving finances, clients, and employees.

Ideally, I would have relied during this time on the counsel and wisdom of my father. That wasn't an option. The day my dad sold his company to me, he hopped on a plane to Southern California to begin a six-month-long backpacking journey through the western United States.

As a new business owner, the only direction I had — the only North Star I could set my eyes upon — was the behavior I had observed from my father during his years of owning and running this business. After working there with him for ten years, I knew our clients, our operations, our employees, and our vision.

I didn't know how to navigate the pressure of being responsible for making hard choices. I didn't know what the company meant to my father beyond a means to earn a living. So, I didn't know how to define what the company meant to me.

All that I knew to do was to emulate the behavior I had observed. My whole life, I saw my father making extraordinary sacrifices to lead and grow his company successfully. Many mornings, he left for work before I got up. Many nights he came home well after I had gone to sleep. In our house, we understood Dad wouldn't be able to make every soccer game, dance recital, and school play.

All I knew was that Dad worked hard, and Dad worked a lot. So, that's what I did. I hardly did anything besides work.

The irony is that 2019, the year I had the unforgettable early morning phone call with John, was the most profitable year in our company's history. I didn't need to be working so much. What I couldn't understand when I woke up at 4:00 a.m. to answer John's phone call was how *not* to do that. Yes, I could have simply looked at the profit-and-loss statement and recognized that we were making enough money to survive a reduced workload on the owner's part. However, my decision to work tirelessly was not a logical one. I was pursuing an aim I had never agreed to.

I realized then that I needed a challenge that would force me to step outside the business. Later that night, I saw a video of a man named Noel Mulkey from Tulsa, Oklahoma, training for an Ironman triathlon. For those unfamiliar, an Ironman triathlon is a 2.4-mile swim followed by a 112-mile bike ride, topped off with an entire 26.2-mile marathon run.

As I saw the video, my first thought was, "I could never imagine doing a race even half that long." I was no endurance athlete. My only experience at the time was begrudgingly running a couple of local YMCA fun-run 5k races back in high school. But my second thought came quickly after the first — "That's exactly the challenge I'm looking for."

The goal was the perfect recipe for balancing out my life, as the magnitude would force me to set aside enough time to have two, sometimes three, workouts in a day for the following year. This meant my business needed to survive without my relentless, round-the-clock attention. I would need to trust my employees with day-to-day decisions, remove distractions from my life, and set clear boundaries with family, friends, and clients. So, I blocked out every training session on my calendar religiously.

Almost immediately, life tested my resolve. I noticed a client meeting on my calendar that directly conflicted with a training run I had scheduled for that evening. So, I walked over to my assistant, Cinthia, and said, "What's going on here?"

"They said they can only meet after 6:00 p.m.," she replied. "They aren't the only ones that say that, either."

A 90-minute meeting starting at 6:00 p.m. meant wrapping up at 7:30 p.m., spending thirty minutes on notes, and driving forty-five minutes back home with barely enough time to eat dinner before 9:00 p.m. There was no chance of a training run that night.

The old Sanger would have sacrificed anything to be present for a client meeting, no matter the time or distance. But I made a choice at that moment. "Please reschedule so I can focus on what was already on the calendar. From now on, I won't see any meetings after 4:30 p.m. Hard stop."

I was terrified. For the next few weeks, I thought I had made a terrible mistake. Sometimes I would lie in bed at night and count how many clients I could afford to lose before I'd have to open my calendar back up again. I'd lie there and sweat gallons, convincing myself I was being selfish and short-sighted. Was a silly race worth derailing everything two generations of men in my family had built?

What happened next was like magic. Clients who, for years, could never meet before dinner time suddenly could see me during lunch hour or in the mornings. Once I aligned myself toward a clear aim and dedicated myself to my mission, people respected that.

I began my grueling training program, dedicating every second of my free time toward running, swimming, riding the bike, stretching, rehabbing sore muscles, weight training, and figuring out how to eat enough clean food to get the 6,000 calories I easily burned on a weekend training ride.

I no longer spent Saturdays with friends and family. Instead, I regularly rode my bike for eight hours, starting at my home in Fort Worth, heading to the town of Mineral Wells forty-five miles away, then turning around and riding right back. Returning home never felt good, either. All it meant was that I now had to put on my running shoes and do laps around the neighborhood until my calves turned to jelly.

I said no to a lot during this time. No to hanging out with friends. No to eating junk food. No to staying up late. No to sleeping in. Most importantly, I said no to my unhealthy relationship with work and my business.

On October 2, 2021, I finished Ironman Indiana in Muncie. Three weeks later, on October 23, 2021, I lined up to race Ironman Waco ninety miles south of my home and office in Fort Worth. My family, several friends, and many employees came to cheer me on. That day, I kept my body moving for fourteen hours straight. I battled frigid water temperatures in the swim, a wetsuit that chafed my arms, flat tires on the bike ride, severe cramps on the run, and blisters on my feet throughout.

The sun was barely rising that morning when I hopped in the Brazos River to start the swim. By the time the finish line was within my sights, the sun had long ago set. People lined either side of the running path behind metal barricades for hundreds of yards leading up to the red tape. Loud, upbeat music pumped through the speakers. Every bystander was whooping and hollering. The entire scene is purposefully designed to honor the athletes' accomplishments with as much fanfare as possible. It was all set up to make me feel like a celebrity. It was designed to make me feel proud. To make me feel strong. To make me feel accomplished.

Over the speakers, the announcer's booming voice called out, "Sanger Smith from Fort Worth: YOU are an Ironman!"

When my shoes crossed the finish line, I didn't feel what I had expected. For the past eleven months, I had dreamt of the moment that would produce pure joy, exuberance, pride, and ecstasy. I didn't feel those things.

Instead, I felt nothing for a moment — and then I felt loss.

Before the race volunteers could even congratulate me, I thought, "Now, what am I going to do on Monday?" Usually, every weekend, I looked forward to tackling my training plan. Suddenly, for the first time in a year, I didn't have one.

But, as soon as I saw my family, friends, and employees, I recognized the meaning of what I had been aiming toward. These people mattered to me far more than a plastic medal. And I had inspired them.

The significance of completing the goal I set for myself differed from the personal achievement. The significance was nothing less than being an example to the people close to me, showing them and myself that they can do more than they may initially think — that we can push farther than we give ourselves credit for.

I do not know where my Ironman medal is, but my red and black Specialized Shiv Sport triathlon bike hangs on the wall in my living room because it was with me every day. What gave this all meaning was the transformational change along the journey, embodied by the representation of the bike. What really matters if your life has significance and meaning?

FINDING SIGNIFICANCE ON A MOUNTAIN TOP

Every summer, I drive to Colorado to hike the 14,000-foot summit mountains. In 2017, a month before my twenty-third birthday, I was hiking one of the shortest routes, Mount Sherman. Though a shorter route, Mount Sherman is still, by any standard of measurement, a true mountain with a summit at 14,043 feet elevation. Normally, I wouldn't be particularly thrilled to climb a relatively easy route, but today, ice covered the mountain, presenting an exciting challenge and a new level of difficulty.

While there, I met Dale. Dale's very presence humbled me immediately. His gray hair and crooked posture looked as out of place on this rugged trail as a kite flying in a library. If there was such a thing as handicapped parking this deep in the wilderness, Dale would have qualified for it based on the stiffness of his back alone. Dale looked athletic in the sense that, perhaps, maybe he had met an athlete once thirty years ago.

I fancied myself a strong, athletic adventurer who sought to conquer one of the tallest points in the American West while Dale stared back at me, a wrinkled, scraggly bearded retired man whose steel rod for a spine reduced his gait to a shuffle. To top it off, Dale carried a snowboard on his back. It was the start of summer. The time for snowboarding had long passed by this point.

Both of us were alone. In silent agreement, we chose to walk together to keep each other company. "Man, my knees are on fire," I broke the silence after a half mile, enduring the embarrassment of complaining in the presence of a man far removed from the youth I had on my side yet still carrying an added twenty pounds.

"You're telling me," Dale said, never taking his eyes off the path under his feet. "I've got arthritis."

When I thought my ego couldn't possibly be bruised more, Dale reminded me that not only was he triple my age, but he had an actual medical reason to move slowly, unlike me.

We powered over boulders for hours, lifting our knees to our chests to carry our bodies over jagged rocks. Every step, every single placement of a foot, was a life-or-death decision. A slight slip on an icy rock could easily break an ankle and leave either of us stranded overnight in freezing temperatures. Halfway to the summit, we reached a long, steep stretch of the mountain completely covered in snow. The only path forward was directly up along a glass mountain, slippery and unforgiving. No footsteps were visible in the tightly packed snow ahead of us, meaning Dale and I were the only ones foolish enough to attempt the ascent. I sat down, slung my pack off my shoulders, and made the only logical decision I knew possible — strap on my steel micro spikes to the soles of my hiking boots for traction. After gearing up, I lifted my chin and saw Dale halfway up the wall with the same shoes he'd been wearing all day.

I was struggling. I couldn't understand what motivated Dale to keep pushing. But, as we hiked, I couldn't help but feel a sense of awe and respect for this man who was determined to reach the summit, no matter what obstacles he faced.

After a long day of hiking, we reached the summit within a minute of each other, exhausted but victorious. No longer concerned with being 'polite' and downright stunned by Dale's effort, I blurted out, "Hey man, what the heck is the snowboard for? There's not even enough snow to use it."

I didn't expect the profound answer I received.

Dale stayed silent for a moment, staring across the mountain tops of central Colorado. Then he finally answered.

"My son."

Knowing there was more to the story, I gave Dale the space to share.

"This is where I taught him to snowboard," he went on. "He loved it here. He'd always beg me to come back, so we made it an annual tradition on his birthday. He died three years ago. But I keep coming."

Hearing his words, I felt a lump form in my throat. I couldn't imagine the pain and loss he must have felt, and yet here he was, pushing through his struggles to honor his son's memory. I felt humbled and inspired by his determination and strength.

Descending from the summit, we parted ways as Dale picked up the pace, and I walked down the rocks alone. I met, that day, a man who had found significance behind his goals. He wasn't climbing a mountain for fun, for the sake of climbing a mountain, or to impress his friends. In fact, he was probably as surprised as I was to see anyone else crazy enough to hike that far that day.

Dale wasn't there that day to snowboard. He wasn't only there that day to hike. He wasn't even there to enjoy the beautiful views from the peak. He was hiking to prove to himself that he still embodied the values he had instilled in his son — the love of nature, the acceptance of difficult challenges, the joy of uncommon journeys, and the desire to push a body to its limits. Hearing his story made my quest seem insignificant. What was the bigger purpose of my hike?

I struggled to reach the top, while Dale never voiced a concern because he had an aim bigger than the mountain itself.

It's the same with every area of our lives. Isn't our relationship with our work enhanced when it means something more than simply drawing a paycheck? Aren't our relationships with our families deeper when they involve something more than simply hanging out together? But, of course, this is true with our financial objectives, too.

If you are saving up money for the sake of having a large account balance, you will never have enough motivation when it's no longer fun and easy to save. However, if you find deeper meaning for what that money can do, no amount of market fluctuation can slow you down. If you, like Dale, have a noble aim for your objectives, then slick, snowy trails, cold winds, and achy knees will not slow you down — even if your pack is heavier than most.

COLOSSIANS 3:23-24

CHAPTER 3

Choosing a *New Path*

> *"Each dream you leave behind is a part of your future that will no longer exist." — Steve Jobs*

A couple of years ago, a prospective client named Kirby was sitting in the lobby of my office building, which is a modern, new-age building in a luxury shopping district of Fort Worth. When I greeted him in the lobby, he looked oddly out of place, dressed casually rather than in professional attire. I learned later that he hadn't stepped foot in an office building in three years. He had gained a few pounds since retiring from the architecture firm where he was a partner, and none of his dress slacks fit anymore. As I approached, he looked almost hopeless.

We sat down in my office, and I asked, "So, what brings you in today?"

Expressionless, Kirby answered in a monotone voice, "I already have a financial advisor. I just want to get your opinion on something."

Most of my clients come to me having already had a relationship with a financial advisor in the past. I thought, "There must be some reason Kirby isn't satisfied with what his current advisor is doing." I was interested. "That's what I do — give my opinion. Let's hear it."

"I've been retired for a few years now," he said as he slid his account statements across the table. "I'm confident I've got enough money to get by and live a nice life, but I'm bored. I want to know if you think I should pull some of this money out and start a coffee shop," he said to me, almost as if he knew he had hardly given enough information to elicit a thoughtful response.

I tried to hold back the slight grin on my face. I wasn't laughing at him; I was instantly excited for this man I barely knew. I was excited because he was beginning to explore the significance of his wealth. "Well, Kirby," I said with a raised eyebrow, "I guess that depends on a lot of things."

I rolled my chair over to the whiteboard and popped the cap off a marker. "It depends on what kind of coffee shop you want yours to be. It depends on the competition in the area you're looking at. It depends on if you really want to be a business owner. It depends on how much time you want to spend working. It depends on a lot. So, I guess the real question is, why is owning a coffee shop important to you?"

I could tell by his stunned expression that no one had asked him that question before. He had the typical reaction one does when faced with examining the importance of one's pursuit. "Because I like coffee."

"Ha-ha," I replied — now I *was* laughing at him — "that can't be it! You can buy all the coffee you want. What's important to you about owning a coffee shop?"

He paused for a moment to think and, with his thumb, flicked the pen he was holding in his right hand. "I always wanted to own a business. I never did. I want to have a positive impact on the lives of the people in my community. The best way I can think of to do that is to be a servant leader and improve the lives of employees and customers."

"So, why aren't you doing that?"

"Well, my advisor keeps telling me I don't need that risk. I'm already successfully retired; I don't need to make more money."

Kirby's advisor was missing the point entirely. Kirby's advisor allowed his own personal values and interest to get in the way of giving Kirby the advice and encouragement he needed.

Most financial advisors are risk-averse. That's usually a good thing. You wouldn't want your advisor to be the type to make big gambles and bet on crazy chances. But, sometimes, people need an opportunity to realize their own version of significance. Kirby found an aim, but his advisor couldn't see the point. His advisor couldn't see the point in taking risks because his advisor lived in a world where goal achievement is the highest good. Kirby's advisor spent his time in a company and industry that teaches people that retiring from a job is the ultimate aim. Kirby knew there was more to life and created a bigger aim. The aim was to build a business that expressed Kirby's love for coffee and for people, each in its fullest possible form.

Kirby and I spent the next hour game-planning the start of his coffee company, building a business plan.

WHAT DREAMS HAVE YOU LEFT BEHIND?

Oddly, the conversation with Kirby opened my eyes to relationships where I acted more like the advisor Kirby fired than the advisor Kirby hired when he met me. So, the next morning, I called Chris and apologized.

Chris had spent his entire career teaching high school math in north Texas. While he was working, we would meet and talk about his plans for retirement. As is usually the case with most folks approaching retirement, we discussed investment strategy, whether he was on track to retire at the age he chose, how to coordinate pension and Social Security benefits with systematic withdrawals on his investment portfolio, and how to navigate bigger decisions like refinancing the house and how to protect against the unexpected.

No matter the focus of our meeting, Chris would reference his dream. He would make cheeky comments like, "So, Sanger, do I have enough money to quit my job so I can start my brewery?"

Every time we talked, he mentioned starting a brewery. I got the feeling it wasn't entirely a joke because I asked him once, "Do you really brew your own beer?"

"Oh, yeah," he said. "This guy who lives in my neighborhood — Jerry. Well, I guess he's not just a guy in my neighborhood, he's a friend, but anyway — Jerry taught me how to brew beer a few years ago, so that's what we do."

Chris had a genuine passion for this hobby Jerry taught him. And suddenly, I knew I had been failing Chris. I failed Chris because, by the time I met Kirby, Chris had been retired for two full years. Both Chris and I knew he had let himself go. It was hard not to see it. He gained weight, stopped getting regular haircuts, stopped shaving, and entirely stopped caring how he dressed.

But now, it was clear to me. This disheveled look wasn't the image of a man breaking free, finally, from the restrictive, but-toned-up environment of a schoolteacher role. This was the im-age of a man genuinely depressed. He was depressed because he no longer had a purpose.

When he was teaching high school math every day, he at least had a purpose in life. On some days, it was a purpose he didn't much care for, yet it was still a purpose. Unfortunately, I had failed to encourage Chris post-retirement to continue to chase his dream of owning a brewery. My job as his ad-visor was not to guide him to a tunnel-visioned end goal but to give him the tools and wisdom necessary to put his money to its highest and best use. My job was to encourage Chris to set his sights on the highest aim imaginable with his money and move diligently, consistently, and steadfastly toward that.

YOUR GOALS ARE NOT THE AIM

Before I picked up the phone that morning to call Chris, I re-alized that achieving so-called goals for the sake of achieving goals is falling miles short of the mark. We don't have that phi-losophy in any other area of life, at least not logically. Or if we have, we recognize the faults.

If you have ever tried to lose weight, you already understand what I am saying. Have you ever found yourself sitting on your couch, eating junk food you know you shouldn't eat, and sud-denly become conscious of your lazy lifestyle? Most people, at this moment, say to themselves — less articulately than this — "I am not all that I could be. I want to change."

When we try to change, what do we do? We set realistic, achievable goals. For example, "I will lose ten pounds before Christmas." That sounds great. And it is even achievable. Perhaps you have been there and told yourself you would lose ten pounds, and you did it.

Now, what happened over the next two months after Christmas — or whatever self-imposed deadline? Most people gain that weight right back, even quicker than they lost it. That is because when you were sitting, sprawled out on the couch on a Thursday night, looking down at your protruding, ever-growing gut, disgusted with yourself, you were not simply disappointed that you weighed ten pounds more than you "should." You had a higher aim, yet that higher aim was undefined. You yearned to be in better physical condition.

I had this exact moment. Thankfully, it happened early in life. I worked on a Texas longhorn ranch during my sophomore year of college. No, not the school in Austin — an actual cattle ranch that raised elite showcase cattle highly sought after by breeders and collectors.

Working on a ranch is demanding work. Each day for lunch, I drove to the local diner and scarfed down a triple cheeseburger. Next, I'd drink a large Dr. Pepper in about three gulps, get a quick refill, then head back over to bail hay, build fences, or whatever other grueling manual labor needed to be done that day.

There isn't a ranch hand alive that isn't a borderline alcoholic, so every day after work, I would meet up with Derek, the other hand, and we'd crush a six-pack of Lonestar — proudly Texas' trashiest light beer.

I put on a solid twenty pounds in one semester. Then, one night I was out with some classmates, and one of my buddies snapped a picture to document the night. I looked over at his phone after he took it and, before I could think, blurted out, "There's no *way* I look like *that*!"

But I did look like that. And I wasn't proud of it. I was simultaneously fat from the beer and skinny from skipping the gym for who knows how long. I didn't look fit at all, and it embarrassed me. Strangely, a more deeply cutting memory played in my head at that exact moment.

I remembered Christmas morning with my father when I was five years old. You know, that age when Dad is still God and Superman and could totally play for the Dallas Cowboys if he wanted to. I sat on the hardwood floor of our living room next to the Christmas tree, opening presents. I got new gloves for Tae Kwon Do. Dad gave me a familiar command, "Give me your best shot," and flexed his arm, exposing his shoulder, goading me to punch him as hard as I could.

"Whoa, Dad, your arms are huge!"

Remembering that moment, I decided on an aim that was bigger than myself. It became as big an aim as a college sophomore could have. I would not rob my future son of believing, if only for a few short years, that I could bench press an eighteen-wheeler if the situation called for it. My aim, therefore, was to become physically fit enough to impress my future son one day on Christmas morning. And it was highly effective. A simple goal of "going to the gym more," "losing ten pounds," or "bench pressing a new personal record" would not have sustained a lifestyle change that persists to this day.

Unfortunately, Chris had lost sight of the aim in place of the goal. And it was my fault.

Since that call with Chris that morning, he has opened his humble brewery in his town. He lights up a room now. He carries himself with pride. He got a haircut.

The old way of doing business as a financial advisor is dying, and I am happy to help guide it to hospice. Most financial advisors do what I did with Chris; they talk to their clients a couple of times a year and tell them they are on the right track. If the client isn't on the right track, they assign a couple of quick prescriptions and leave the client to their own devices to figure out how to implement these steps. They have a "you should" philosophy — they'll point you in the right direction, but they won't walk with you.

Kirby and Chris inspired me to make a renewed commitment. As an advisor, I am both legally and morally obligated to give you advice that is in your best interest. To do that well, I must have more frequent meetings and be as involved as possible.

JEREMIAH 29:11

CHAPTER 4

How Long Are You Going to *Wait?*

"Don't underestimate the hole your absence would leave."
— Dr. Jordan B. Peterson

M eeting with a wealth advisor can leave you feeling vulnerable in the same way as hiring a personal trainer after avoiding stepping foot in a gym for the past decade. It's tempting to soothe ourselves with the comforting lie, "I'll talk to a professional once I get a little more organized" or "... once I save a little more money" or "... once I sell the business" or "... after we buy this house." It's easy to postpone professional guidance until things are just right. Unfortunately, things never are exactly right.

The very day Marci's bank account showed, for the first time, more commas and zeros than she ever thought she'd have to her name was the worst day of her financial life.

Marci and her husband, Mark, were the type of couple that lived as one united flesh. It was impossible for anyone who ever knew either Mark or Marci to imagine one without the other. Any time I saw Mark, I saw Marci. Any time I saw Marci, I saw Mark with her. The story was true whether we were at church, the golf course, or a dinner party.

Marci is a dedicated mother who sacrificed a promising career as an attorney to stay home to raise their kids. Mark, meanwhile, owned a manufacturing company for decades. He always told me, "I know I need to come and see you and talk money," but he never did. He'd always follow up his proclamation with a qualification: "It's the busy season right now," or "Once we get cash flow straightened out." After several years, it turned into "Once I sell the business."

Ultimately, Mark never came to see me. He passed away in a car accident. And so, with no knowledge of running a manufacturing company, Marci became the owner overnight.

Several months after Mark's accident, Marci and I met at her and Mark's favorite lunch spot overlooking the Trinity River. She was smiling again despite weeks of grieving for her lost husband. Before my butt could touch the seat, she exclaimed, "I sold the business!"

"That's great news, Marci," I replied, trying to sound supportive despite my concerns about her lack of knowledge of the business world. "How did the sale go?"

Marci's smile faded slightly as she explained that the sale had been a rushed and stressful process. A group of investors had approached her about buying the machinery inside the warehouse, and she had agreed to sell it to them for a sum she thought was fair. I was heartbroken for Marci. Selling the machinery for cash was undoubtedly better than trying to run a business about which she had no knowledge. Still, she left an unbelievable amount of money on the table by not selling the business.

I wished she had come and spoken to me sooner. I would have done for her what I've done for so many clients: walk them through the long, sometimes complicated process of selling their business and achieving maximum value at sale price.

"I had no idea how much the business or the machinery was worth," Marci admitted, looking down at her hands. "I just wanted to get it all over with as quickly as possible. I guess I was embarrassed that I didn't know anything, so I figured I'd just get it done on my own when the investors approached me," she said shyly, knowing that I would have been happy to help.

I nodded sympathetically, understanding the overwhelming burden Marci must have felt after the sudden loss of her husband and the responsibility of managing the business. "Well, how much did they pay for the equipment?" I asked.

When Marci told me the number, my heart sank. I didn't need fancy charts, graphs, or even a basic calculator to know that would not be enough to sustain her spending throughout her life. It is understandable that Marci wanted to move on as quickly as possible and thought professional advice would drag out that grieving process. I even understand why Mark, while he was alive, continued to delay seeking professional guidance. Like the rest of us, he thought he had plenty of time.

Marci looked at me with a mixture of sadness and regret. "I wish Mark had come to see you before all this happened," she said quietly. "I know he always meant to, but he kept putting it off. And now it's too late."

The right exit planning advisor could have helped Mark and Marci understand the full value of the machinery and the business and negotiate a better sale price, maximizing the return for their family. It would have meant Marci never needed to work again a day in her life, their two sons could go to college without debt, and the family could contribute substantially to their church. The right exit planning advisor could have set Mark up with an exit strategy years ago; a buy-sell agreement with existing company employees that would pay Marci out if Mark passed and the proper risk protection plans to cover his family if he passed away unexpectedly. The reality Marci now faces is bleaker than that, unfortunately. She works in the office of a local attorney as a receptionist. She'll keep doing that for another fifteen years, at least.

WHAT IS HOLDING YOU BACK?

As a private wealth advisor, I have seen firsthand the profound consequences of neglecting to seek professional guidance when making critical financial decisions. Mark and Marci's story exemplify the disastrous impact of inaction. Mark's reluctance to consult with a professional forced Marci and their sons to pay a price bigger than they could have imagined.

In today's world, we are bombarded with an abundance of information, making it difficult to discern whom to trust. It is all too easy to succumb to confirmation bias and seek information that aligns with our preexisting beliefs or goals. However, it is vital to make the time to thoroughly comprehend our options and seek professional guidance to ensure that we make informed and wise decisions. Not only wise decisions but decisions that align with our values. Mark deeply and profoundly loved his family. Leaving them destitute without a plan for a better future was certainly not in alignment with his values, yet that is the reality they face.

Having financial goals is essential, but understanding the motivations behind your goals is more important. What do you want your money to represent to you, your family, and those who will ultimately steward your money long after you leave this earth? By working with a professional and explicitly shining a light on your values, you can make decisions that align with your goals and the tenets of human existence that are most important to you.

Mark's decision to delay seeking professional guidance not only cost his family a significant amount of money but also left them with no comprehension of the significance of the money they inherited. Marci was left to navigate the business sale independently, without the knowledge and resources necessary to make informed decisions. It is crucial to remember that professional guidance is not solely about maximizing financial returns but also about gaining the understanding and knowledge required to make informed decisions about your own finances and future so you can live the life you imagine for yourself and your family.

Common Reasons People Hesitate to Seek Advice

People might put off speaking with a wealth advisor for one of many reasons:

- **Information overload:** They feel overwhelmed by the amount of information available and don't know where to turn for help.
- **Lack of knowledge:** They feel like they don't know enough about money to determine which advisor is best for them.
- **Lack of time:** They have busy lives and just don't want to focus on it, thinking, "I don't have the time to worry about that right now."

Understandably, people may feel these things, but it's important to remember that seeking professional guidance is an essential step in making your money mean the most that it can.

Just as you might put off going to see a doctor about chest pain until it becomes unbearable, some people put off seeking financial advice until they are in a dire situation. Regular checkups with a doctor can prevent health problems before they become serious. So, too, can regular financial planning conversations prevent money problems before they become overwhelming. Something may be wrong that only shows up on an X-ray. We cannot be the healthiest we can be without health advice. Likewise, we cannot be the wealthiest we can be without wealth advice.

To be the wealthiest we can be does not mean to have the largest account balance possible. Instead, it means to apply our abundant resources purposefully toward the good in the best way we are capable of.

Seeking professional guidance doesn't have to be intimidating or time-consuming. A good wealth advisor will collaborate with you to develop a personalized financial plan that considers your uniqueness. They can help you understand your options and make informed decisions about your money, so you can achieve success *and* significance.

THE GIFT OF DOING GOOD

Barbara was a soft-spoken divorcee who lived in my neighborhood. I had the pleasure of meeting her by chance one day as I was out for a walk. She struck me as a kind and gentle soul, and I was immediately drawn to her. As it turned out, she eventually became a client of mine.

At first, Barbara wasn't interested in engaging in any conversations with me outside of her investment account. Whenever I tried to delve deeper and discuss what mattered to her, she deflected the conversation to the happenings in our neighborhood or her weekend plans. It was hard to put a finger on why such a warm, open person would shut off so quickly to these conversations, but I was determined to gain her trust and help her do more with her money.

As I got to know Barbara better, I discovered she was incredibly generous, with a big heart. She loved to volunteer and was passionate about a few local organizations that did outstanding work. She was particularly fond of the Gary Sinise Foundation.

"I just love the work they do," Barbara told me one day as we sat in my office. "They do so much to support military members and their families. Since my dad was in the Navy, I want to do anything I can to support them."

I listened intently as Barbara spoke, struck by her passion and dedication. I clearly understood that her wealth meant more to her than just a financial asset. She wanted to use it to positively impact the world and leave a lasting legacy.

Determined to help Barbara achieve this, I persisted in my efforts to understand what was truly important to her regarding her money. Through our conversations and thorough financial planning, we developed a plan to transform her wealth into something genuinely significant: a trust to fund the charities she cared about and a legacy for her family to continue her impactful work.

"I never thought about my wealth in this way before," Barbara said with a sense of wonder. "But now I feel like it has a purpose, a significance that goes beyond financial security."

It wasn't always easy to get Barbara to open up about what mattered most to her, but I'm so glad we could do the work together. It was a genuine pleasure to see the joy and purpose that our planning brought to her life. Sadly, a few short months after we established the trust, Barbara unexpectedly passed away in her sleep. While it was a difficult and unexpected loss, I took comfort in knowing that Barbara's wealth would continue to make a positive impact on the world through the charities she cared about, helping military families like the one she grew up in, and that her family could carry on her legacy of generosity and kindness.

THE NEXT GENERATION OF PHILANTHROPY

After Barbara's unexpected passing, her daughters inherited the trust we had set up together. At first, the sudden responsibility overwhelmed them, and they were not entirely sure what to do with the wealth their mother had left them. But as they delved into the work of the charities their mother supported, they began to find their own sense of purpose and significance.

As they got to know the people who benefited from their mother's generosity, they were struck by the profound impact their mother's wealth had made on those people's lives. Inspired by their mother's legacy, Barbara's daughters explored other ways they could use their wealth to make a difference. They worked with me to develop a plan that would allow them to support causes that were important to them in making a positive impact on the world.

As they delved deeper into this work, they, too, discovered that their wealth had the power to do more than provide financial security. It could change lives and make the world a better place. And in doing so, they found a sense of significance and purpose that went beyond anything they could have imagined.

FEAR FACTORS

Three primary fear factors prevent people from transforming their wealth to significance. These fears often revolve around questions of financial security and uncertainty, and they can be challenging to overcome.

1. *Fear of not having enough money to meet our current daily needs.*

In particular, this fear can acutely affect those in the early phase of their careers or who have previously experienced financial setbacks. It's natural to worry about whether we have enough money to cover our current expenses and enjoy the things we want in life.

2. *Fear of not having enough money to cover our future needs.*

Concerns about retirement, unexpected expenses, or the possibility of a financial emergency can drive this fear. It's understandable to worry about whether we have enough money saved up to handle these potential challenges.

3. *Fear of not being able to trust the advice we are receiving.*

With so much information available online, knowing whom to trust about financial matters can be challenging. Therefore, it's important to do our due diligence and work with advisors who have a proven track record of success and integrity.

Overcoming these fear factors is essential if we want to transform our wealth to significance. It's not easy, but by taking the time to understand our values and priorities, seeking professional guidance, and developing a plan that aligns with our goals, we can find a sense of purpose and meaning in our wealth beyond only financial security.

ISAIAH 41:10

CHAPTER 5

The Decision Lab *Process*

"Without God, life has no purpose, and without purpose, life has no meaning. Without meaning, life has no significance or hope."
— Rick Warren, *"The Purpose Driven Life: What on Earth Am I Here for?"*

THE 5 KEY DECISIONS

As a private wealth advisor and the founder of a wealth management firm, I have spent my career helping people transform their wealth to significance. And over the years, I have developed a proprietary approach I call the Decision Lab process.

We designed this process to help clients build the right financial plan, one that is customized and truly transforms their wealth to significance. The fundamental principle of this process is to take clients through the "5 Key Decisions," each of which will create opportunities for other decisions that all help clients make the most of their wealth.

Foundationally, the five most important decisions you will make in your financial life are these.

1. *Decide who you are.*

Take time to understand your values and priorities. What makes you who you are? Figure out what matters most to you and what you want your wealth to accomplish.

2. *Decide where you are.*

Gain understanding of your current financial situation, including your assets, debts, and income. Know where you stand and which tools you have at your disposal.

3. *Decide where you are going.*

Set clear financial objectives and develop a plan to achieve them. Figure out what you want your wealth to accomplish in the short term, the long term, and beyond.

4. *Decide how to get there.*

Choose the right financial strategies and tools to help you reach your goals. Figure out the steps you need to take and the resources you need to achieve your objectives.

5. *Decide who matters.*

Identify the people and organizations most important to you and determine how your wealth can support them. Decide whom you want to leave a legacy for and how it can positively impact the world.

You can use these five key decisions to break down everything in life. It doesn't matter what you're trying to accomplish. Whether you want to build a successful business, create a happy family, or achieve personal fulfillment, these five decisions are the key to the success and fulfillment you deserve.

SARAH'S BAKERY

Years ago, I used the 5 Key Decisions process to help a friend, Sarah, build her dream business. Sarah had always dreamed of starting her own bakery, but she needed to figure out how to make it a reality.

She started by looking at the first key decision: deciding who she was. Sarah was a talented baker with a passion for creating delicious pastries and cakes. She was also a hard worker and a natural leader, able to inspire and motivate her team.

Next, she looked at the second key decision: deciding where she was. Sarah worked as a pastry chef at a local restaurant, but she was ready to start her own business. She had saved up some money and had a strong network of contacts in the food industry. She needed to figure out how to turn those resources into a successful bakery.

For the third key decision, Sarah decided where she wanted to go. She dreamed of opening a small bakery in a popular neighborhood and of using organic, locally sourced ingredients. In addition, she wanted to create a warm, welcoming atmosphere where people could enjoy a delicious breakfast or lunch or pick up a treat for a special occasion.

To achieve her goals, she needed to decide and plan how to get there, which was the fourth key decision. First, Sarah worked to create a business plan, including a detailed budget, marketing strategy, and timeline. She also identified potential obstacles and devised a plan to overcome them.

Finally, she looked at the fifth key decision: deciding who mattered. Sarah knew she couldn't do it alone and needed a team of dedicated and talented people to help her achieve her dreams. She also knew that her family and friends would be a crucial support system. She needed to make time for them even as she worked to build her business. Beyond that, and most importantly, she wanted to make sure that young adults with disabilities had an opportunity to earn a dignified living. For Sarah, *they* are the people who matter most.

Using the 5 Key Decisions process, Sarah turned her dream of starting a bakery into a reality. She opened her doors to a warm reception, and her business has been thriving, employing young adults with down syndrome and autism. She credits the 5 Key Decisions process with helping her focus on what mattered most and make the right choices along the way.

SIGNIFICANCE AFTER A BUSINESS SALE

I had the pleasure of working with a client, Jack, who had recently sold his successful technology company. Jack had worked hard to build his business from the ground up and was proud of everything he had accomplished. But now that he had sold the company, he was unsure what to do next.

We started by looking at the first key decision: deciding who he was. Jack was a natural entrepreneur with a passion for innovation and a desire to make a difference in the world. He was also a devoted husband and father with a keen sense of family values.

Next, we looked at the second key decision: deciding where he was. Jack had sold his business for a significant sum of money, and he had many options. He could retire, invest in other companies, or start a new venture. He needed to figure out which path to follow.

For the third key decision, we decided on where Jack wanted to go. He told me he wanted to use his wealth to make a positive impact on the world and to create a legacy for his family. He wanted to do something meaningful and fulfilling that benefited the city he lived in, but he wasn't sure what that meant for him.

To achieve his aim, we needed to plan — deciding how to get there. Jack's impact could live beyond his natural life if he left explicit instructions. So, we built a legacy plan that clearly articulated who would receive the money and how, in his absence, his family would direct the wealth toward those areas he felt deserved the most aid.

Finally, we looked at the fifth key decision: deciding who mattered. Jack knew that his family would be a crucial part of his legacy and that he wanted to involve them in his plans. So, instead of naming his foundation after himself, he named it after his children, motivating them to continue his legacy of philanthropy.

We spent some time discussing different charitable organizations and causes that were meaningful to Jack, and he eventually created a foundation to support education and technology initiatives. He also set up a trust for his children, which would help teach them the importance of giving back and making a difference in the world.

With the 5 Key Decisions process, Jack transformed his wealth to significance. He found a sense of purpose and fulfillment that he had never experienced before, and he created a legacy that would benefit his family and the world. He credits the 5 Key Decisions process with helping him to focus on what matters most and make the right choices along the way.

ADOLFO AND THE PAPER COMPANY

Adolfo had been running a successful paper company, Campbell Paper, for years and was planning to sell. However, he had been diagnosed with a terminal illness and knew he wouldn't be able to run the company for much longer. In addition, Adolfo had no children, so selling was the only option he had to set up his wife for financial security moving forward.

I reached out to him, offering my services as an advisor, but he politely declined, stating that he had done his research and felt confident in handling the sale on his own.

A few months went by, and I received a call from Adolfo. His usually strong voice was filled with desperation and regret. He had closed the sale of Campbell Paper for $10 million, and now he realized the magnitude of his mistakes.

"My accountant is saying I owe a ton of money in taxes now," he said.

I met Adolfo at his office, and he filled me in on the terms of the sale. Unfortunately, the buyer had written Adolfo a check upfront, meaning Adolfo was responsible for paying taxes on the full $10 million. This resulted in a significant tax bill, leaving Adolfo with only a little more than $6 million after everything was said and done.

Furthermore, the buyer had included a non-compete clause in the sale agreement, preventing Adolfo from working as a consultant for any similar paper company for the next five years. This limited his earning potential and removed any ability to recoup the money lost in taxes through part-time work as a consultant. The buyer had clearly said they would not hire Adolfo in any role.

Adolfo could have used a charitable remainder unitrust (CRUT) to avoid some of the taxes associated with the sale of his business. A CRUT is a type of trust that provides an income stream to the grantor, in this case Adolfo and his wife, for a specified period, then distributes the remaining assets to a charitable organization.

By transferring ownership of his company to a CRUT, Adolfo could have avoided paying taxes on the full $10 million sale price. Instead, he would have only been taxed on the income generated by the trust, which would have been a fraction. Additionally, he could have benefited from an immediate tax deduction for a portion of the value of the assets transferred to the trust.

After Adolfo and his wife passed on, the remaining assets would have been distributed to the charitable organizations they selected. Further, the CRUT would have continued to pay income to both him and his wife throughout their lives.

OTHER STRATEGIES FOR DOING GOOD

Adolfo could have used several other strategies to reduce his tax liability on the sale of his business:

Deferral of income

Adolfo could have structured the sale of his business to include a deferred payment schedule, which would have allowed him to spread the income from the sale over several years. Doing this would have allowed him to defer the taxes on the income until he or his wife received it.

Installment sale

Adolfo could have structured the sale of his business as an installment sale, which would have allowed him to receive payments over some time rather than all at once. Again, spreading the income over several years would also spread the taxes out over those years.

Exchange

Adolfo could have exchanged his shares in Campbell Paper company for shares of the buyer's company, with a clear plan to sell those shares at a predetermined schedule over time. This would also allow Adolfo to avoid a massive tax bomb in the year of the sale.

Donor-advised fund

A donor-advised fund (DAF) is a charitable giving vehicle that allows individuals to make charitable contributions, receive an immediate tax deduction, and then recommend grants to charitable organizations over time.

Let's say that Adolfo sold his company for $10 million and wanted to contribute $1 million to his favorite charities. This would make sense, considering Adolfo was a consistent tither throughout his life. With a DAF, the IRS would have treated the $1 million contribution as if it had gone directly to the charities. This would have allowed him to claim the charitable deduction on his taxes in the same year he received the income from the sale, thus offsetting much of the tax liability.

Further, Adolfo and his wife could have then made grant recommendations over time, thus allowing them to have a more meaningful impact for years, even after his passing.

BENEFITS OF DONOR-ADVISED FUNDS

Immediate Tax Deduction

Contributors to a donor-advised fund (DAF) are eligible to receive an immediate tax deduction based on the fair market value of the assets contributed. The deduction can be claimed in the tax year the contribution is made, and the amount of the tax deduction depends on the individual's tax bracket and the type of assets donated.

Flexibility

With a DAF, donors can contribute a wide range of assets, including cash, publicly traded securities, real estate, and private company stock. This allows donors to diversify their philanthropic portfolios and enjoy the different tax benefits associated with different types of assets.

Simplicity

DAFs are relatively easy to set up and manage. Once the DAF is established, donors can easily make contributions and recommend grants to charitable organizations.

Anonymity

DAFs offer donors the choice to remain anonymous if they wish. This can benefit donors who want to make a charitable contribution without drawing attention to themselves.

Professional Management

DAFs are typically managed by professional staff with knowledge of charitable giving and investment management.

Family Involvement

DAFs can be set up as a family fund, which allows multiple generations of a family to participate in philanthropy and make recommendations for grant-making.

Potential for Future Giving

DAFs are typically set up as irrevocable trusts, meaning the donor cannot receive assets back once they are contributed. However, this also means that the assets in the DAF can continue to grow tax-free, creating a reserve of funds that can be distributed to charitable organizations over time.

JAMES 1:5

CHAPTER 6

Understanding
Your *Values*

"Your core values are the deeply held beliefs that
authentically describe your soul." – John C. Maxwell

So, what is the first step on the path to transforming your wealth to significance? It all starts with a values assessment. It's about getting clear about who you are and what matters deeply to you.

We all have an image of our ideal selves. If you close your eyes and think of the best version of yourself that you could be, there is an image. You know the things about that ideal version of you that matter. You can see what your ideal self does for a living, how they treat other people, how they invest their time, and what aspirations they pursue.

In reality, you are not that ideal self. Not yet. The only things standing between you and that ideal version of who you could be are the choices you make in life. To have any chance of making the right decisions to fulfill that ideal image, you first must know what values subconsciously constructed the image in your mind in the first place.

Whether or not you are aware of them, your deeply held values function as the foundation for your ideal self. Bring those out of the subconscious so they may actively guide your actions, both the big life choices and the day-to-day minutia.

Why is this so important that it is the first step? Because significance looks different for everyone, and to realize it, we have to think beyond daily habits. Our consumerist culture tells us we should spend money on comfort, pleasure, and convenience. Is doing so a mistake? Of course not. Yet, if we only listen to those messages, will that lead to significance in terms of a higher good? No.

To achieve significance, we must think beyond the cultural messages. Contrary to those, money was not designed to be spent only on luxury. As a concept and a tool, it was actually not designed for any particular spending purpose at all. Money exists as a neutral means of asset exchange to eliminate the inefficiencies of a barter system. Your money will come and go from your life without inherent judgment regarding its source or destination. You, meanwhile, have the opportunity — and the responsibility — to decide for yourself where it goes and why. Should you not, therefore, align it with the highest good you wish to achieve?

To do that, the one thing you must get clear on is who you are and what matters deeply to you. This knowledge is vital to making the other four key decisions we discussed in the previous chapter.

For example, how can you possibly know who and what matters to you if you don't even know who you are, what you believe in, and what you want to make happen in the world? Without this self-awareness, it's easy to get caught up in the noise of the outside world and lose sight of what truly matters to *you*.

HOW TO FIND YOUR TRUE VALUES

So, how do you do a values assessment? Start with some introspection. Make time to think about your beliefs, your goals, and your priorities. What are the things that are most important to you? What do you stand for? What do you want to achieve in life? How do you want to be remembered?

Often people make the mistake of believing vague words will do the job of guiding them through life. No. Be as precise as possible about what you want your life to look like. To do this, you need to know exactly what it means to live out your values.

1. Write down as many values as you can think of: for example, "honesty," "wisdom," "beauty," etc.
2. Judge each value based on your first impression of whether it resonates deeply with you. This acts as a quick filter to remove values that cannot make it to your top ten.
3. Narrow it down to fifteen and spread them out on a table so you can see each one. Read the definition of each word.
4. Whittle the list down to ten. This is an excellent opportunity to consolidate similar values, although that's not required. For example, if you have "honesty," "ethics," "morality," and "integrity," you might only need one of these words to grasp what you're aiming toward.
5. Select the top five values that encompass your ideal self.

6. Record your thoughts on what those values mean to you in your own words.
7. Turn these value words into action phrases.
8. Clearly define each phrase, so there will be no confusion in the future when you make big decisions.

Don't overthink it. You may find some phrases in your recording in Step 6 above are precisely the right fit. After all, they are your own words, so they came straight from the heart.

In my company, I found that other people differently interpreted the words I had selected for our core values. For example, I chose integrity as one of our core values, but guess what? People who don't have integrity will never tell you they don't care about integrity as a value. Instead, they interpret it differently to fit within their own worldview. Once I changed our value words into action phrases, the room for misinterpretation disappeared.

Name your values with action-inspiring language. For example, the word "freedom" is vague and different people can interpret it differently. That means even you can interpret it differently at different times, depending on your mood, environment, and other factors.

You don't believe me? Enron — the company infamous for its fraudulent business practices that led to bankruptcy in 2001 — listed "integrity" as one of its core values on its website and in its annual report in 2000. The Enron scandal was one of the largest corporate scandals and audit failures in American history and still is the most widely recognized example of corrupt business practices. Yet, its employees, executive team, and shareholders all believed they were being guided by integrity.

To be precise with your orientation toward the good of your aim, choose language like "be free to be yourself," "exercise discipline to create options," or "follow your own path." Each of these phrases is action-oriented and precisely tells you what living up to the command looks like.

Here's an example:

Decisiveness: "Be firm in character and purpose."

Make decisions quickly and confidently by knowing who you are and the mission you serve.

Servant Leadership: "Lead through service."

Commit to doing what is best for others. Clients and team members will follow you if they know you want what is in their best interest.

Integrity: "Be precise in your speech."

Say what you mean, mean what you say, and honor your word. Speak ideas into existence and harness the power of your voice.

Authenticity: "Have the freedom to be yourself."

Being who you are is the greatest gift you can give the world. Put yourself in environments and relationships that encourage you to exist authentically.

Advancement: "Seek constant progress."

Maintain the highest aim imaginable and commit to improving by 1 percent each day.

LIVING YOUR VALUES

Now that you've completed your values assessment, named your top five values, turned those values into action phrases, and defined each one, it's time to start living up to them in your daily life.

"But, Sanger, how do I make sure that I stay true to my values every day?" Here are a few practical tips to keep you on track.

Keep Your Values Top of Mind

One of the best ways to live up to your values is to write them down and keep them somewhere visible — a sticky note on your computer, on your bathroom mirror, in your wallet, on your phone home screen. Put them where you will see them every day. Each time you see these values, they will remind you of your noble aim. This will mean it's harder to forget your values when emotions inevitably wedge between you and your ideal.

Always Consider Your Values When Making Decisions

When you face a big decision, pause to consider how it aligns with your values. Many people make the mistake of forecasting the outcome of any given decision and justifying that unknown outcome as aligning with their values. This is the wrong approach. Instead, ask yourself this: Does the process by which I concluded this align with what is deeply important to me? How would my ideal self move forward in this scenario? By deciding X, which of my values am I embodying?

Seek Opportunities to Live Your Values

Look for the moments, big and small, in daily life that allow your values to shine the most. This might mean volunteering for a charity that aligns with your values or finding a new job that gives you a chance to be authentically you.

Reflect on Your Choices

After making big choices, take time to evaluate whether your decisions align with your values. If you're not living up to your values as much as you'd like, change and get back on track.

I spoke with former financial executive and entrepreneur Doug Lennick on my podcast. He's the founder of think2perform, a company focused on coaching high-performing executives and athletes on the science and art of elite mental performance. He taught me a clever trick he uses for aligning daily living with his values.

He sets random alarms on his phone that go off at unpredictable times throughout the day. Each alarm calls Doug to stop what he's doing and ask himself three questions. What am I doing? What am I feeling? What am I thinking? In an ideal scenario, Doug's actions, emotions, and thoughts align with his core values. However, when they aren't, he stops what he's doing, reframes his emotions, and changes his thinking.

THE DANGER OF LEAVING YOUR VALUES HIDDEN

Sylvia had always been a diligent saver. And that might be the biggest understatement I could make about her. Throughout her working life, she had relentlessly put money aside every month, rain or shine, determined to have a comfortable retirement. When she finally retired from her job, she lived exclusively off her pension and Social Security benefits. Still, she kept saving her money. Every month. Without fail.

Despite all the hard work saving, Sylvia never got around to making her money do anything for her. She never explored the 5 Key Decisions and, as a result, never knew what was profoundly important to her. I mean, sure, if you asked her, she could answer. She would have said her friends and community were important — she was religiously involved in the local neighborhood watch.

She might have said her church, which she attended every Sunday, was important to her. She might have said the pets she rescued from the shelter, two chocolate labs and a cat named Spoof, were important to her.

Her money decisions didn't illustrate the importance of these things, though. Because she avoided the Decision Lab and the 5 Key Decisions, she never explicitly identified what mattered more than anything else. Worse, she never identified who mattered more than anyone else.

When Sylvia passed away, her money went to her next of kin, who happened to be a distant cousin, as Sylvia had no spouse or children. A solid chunk of it also went to the government in taxes. None of it went to charities or causes that she cared about. None of it went to fund the neighborhood watch. None of it went to the church. None of it went to support animal shelters, either.

I bet Sylvia would have cringed if she could have seen where her money went. The distant cousin was in and out of prison with drug problems, an ailment a hefty sum of money likely made worse. Her other beneficiary, the government, was no friend to a conservative southern woman, either.

SOCIAL CAPITAL

Social capital is the idea that we all have a responsibility to do good for others. Those of us who are blessed with abundant resources have a social obligation to give back to our communities and to make the world a better place.

Now, it doesn't matter whether you agree with the concept of social capital because the government does. And they collect all our social capital when we pay taxes. That money goes to Washington, and the politicians decide for you which causes are important and where your money should go to have the most significant impact.

Like Sylvia, you can leave behind a large sum of money that ends up giving D.C. a big payday and let the politicians decide which causes to fund. Or you can decide.

I believe you have a moral obligation to minimize the taxes you pay by redirecting the wealth that would have gone to the IRS to causes you know to be important. Here's the even better news: the government agrees with me. They want you to choose, which is why they wrote rules into the tax code for you to do that.

TIPS FOR CREATING MORE IMPACT AND SAVING ON TAXES

Charitable Gifts

Any assets you give to a qualified non-profit organization will not be included in your taxable estate. This means you can donate as much as you'd like to charity without worrying about estate taxes on those dollars. Further, you can receive an income tax deduction, too.

Disclaimers by Beneficiaries

Include a disclaimer provision in your will or trust, allowing your beneficiaries to choose to give a part or all their inheritance to a charity. This can be a tax-efficient way to support causes important to your loved ones and to allow them to take part in your legacy of generosity.

Annual Lifetime Gift Limits

You can gift another person a certain amount of assets each year without incurring FIT or estate tax. Over time, this can help reduce the size of your taxable estate and provide financial support to your loved ones.

Charitable Lead Trust

This type of trust supplies an income stream to a charity during your lifetime, and then the assets in the trust will pass on to your beneficiaries after you die. You can structure the trust so your heirs will receive the assets at a specific age. You can set up a maximum zeroed-out charitable lead trust, which eliminates the possibility of income or estate taxes for your heirs.

Charitable Remainder Trust

We discussed this thoroughly in Chapter 6. This strategy allows you to make a large donation now and receive a substantial income-tax deduction while still receiving income from the trust during your lifetime. The assets in the trust will then pass to the charities upon your death.

Qualified Terminable Interest Property (Q-TIP) Trust

A Q-TIP trust can provide income to your spouse after you pass away and then pass the assets in the trust to an irrevocable beneficiary, such as a charity. This allows you to provide for your spouse's well-being while ensuring that the trust assets will go to the beneficiary of your choice.

MATTHEW 22:37-39

CHAPTER 7

Caution Is a *Good Thing*

"If you find yourself in a hole, stop digging."
— *Will Rogers*

As a wealth advisor, my greatest privilege is working with and learning from many families from diverse backgrounds. Each person has a unique story, set of values, and aspirations for their wealth. However, one common thread runs through all my clients: their internal doubts when deciding to hire a wealth advisor.

It is natural to wonder whether a wealth advisor can genuinely understand and help with your specific situation. With something as important as your wealth, it would be foolish of you not to approach this decision with caution. However, some reasons for hesitating spring from false assumptions and unproductive thinking, which only delay progress.

FALSE ASSUMPTIONS AND BELIEFS

A litany of false beliefs regarding wealth management permeates our culture. I've listed a few here.

"All I need is to retire comfortably and pay for medical bills as I get older."

Listen, I get it. You're thinking, "I don't need all this fancy stuff. I just want to retire comfortably and make sure I don't end up in the poorhouse." And that's completely understandable! The wealth management industry has a reputation for focusing on simple, straightforward goal achievement, but that's not all your resources are capable of. A great advisor will specialize in multiplying your impact and implementing a strategy to generate success for every aspect of your future.

Think about it like this — of course, you want to make sure you can retire comfortably and handle any medical expenses that come up. But how would you feel if you could leave a legacy for your loved ones? What would your reaction be if your wealth made a positive impact in your community? What would life look like if you started a business that shared the gift of your values? If managed properly, these are all opportunities that your resources can make possible.

And let me tell you, there's nothing quite like the feeling of achieving your aspirations while simultaneously making a positive impact on the world. So don't sell yourself short by only thinking about retirement and medical expenses. To do so is to dampen the bright light you have within you. To do so is to rob the world of the gift of your existence. With the right advisor, the possibilities are endless.

"Every wealth advisor does the same thing."

As of 2021, there were approximately 330,300 financial advisors in the United States, according to the Bureau of Labor Statistics (BLS).[3] The BLS projects the number to grow by 15 percent by 2031. But let me tell you something: Those hundreds of thousands of advisors are certainly not all out here doing the same thing. It might seem like they all do the same thing on the surface, but there's a substantial difference between the average wealth advisor and a wealth advisor who genuinely cares about you and your aspirations.

See, in the past, many wealth management firms have relied on pushing products and hiring "advisors" to function as salespeople for their packaged investment solutions. A great advisor will act independently of that outdated model. Evaluate the firms and the partners associated with the advisors you interview and see what lies behind the curtain.

Your wealth is the most powerful tool you have, and you should put the responsibility for its investment in the hands of people who understand what matters to you. A great advisor doesn't focus only on surface-level numbers and figures; they will dig deeper to understand what matters to you.

A great advisor will formatively transform wealth planning to go deeper, using your resources to create security for your future, give you the freedom to achieve your aspirations, and leave a lasting impact. If all you're looking for is someone to care about helping you "retire comfortably," you're more likely to run into those advisors who use cookie-cutter solutions and are only in the game to make a quick buck. Instead, the right advisor will help you make the most out of your wealth, so you can truly make a difference in the world, transforming wealth to significance.

"Money is money. My values don't need to be a part of the discussion."

You know, many people have this limiting idea about money. They don't see why their values should have a place at the table in managing it. Unfortunately, even a lot of advisors believe this lie, too.

This couldn't be further from the truth. Every single one of us has a unique set of values and beliefs that drive our decisions, whether or not we're aware of it. In managing your wealth, just as with managing your life, understanding those underlying values is crucial in making the best decisions for yourself and your future. Wealth is simply an abundance of resources. To apply this limited mindset to any other type of resource immediately sounds ridiculous. Imagine being fortunate enough to have plenty of free time and saying, "Eh, time is just time. I don't know why what's important to me has to do with how I manage my time."

I get it — being vulnerable with a financial professional seems uncomfortable. The right advisor, though, will make it easy. Even if you don't know exactly what *is* or what *should be* important to you, a great advisor will guide you through that discovery process and help you identify what matters most. Once you know that, you and your advisor can make sure every financial decision you make aligns with those values. Furthermore, you can make sure your aspirations, aims, and the very core of the significance you seek all align with those values.

When you have a deep understanding of your values, you can live in alignment. Doug Lennick pioneered something called the Alignment Model.[4] It's how he coaches athletes, executives, and high performers on how to live a life aligned at every turn with their core values. This is the key to creating security for yourself and your loved ones, experiencing the freedom to achieve your aspirations, and leaving a lasting impact through the resources you've built. To me, that's what this is all about. That's the real power of aligning your wealth with your values.

In a video on his YouTube channel, Canadian psychologist Jordan B. Peterson said, "Don't underestimate the hole your absence would leave." Every person is a remarkable creature with something to offer loved ones and the world, he explains. "It's our responsibility to make that manifest, and we move a little farther away from paradise every time that doesn't happen."[5]

To live this life without aligning your money decisions to your values means to leave behind, when you die, money that is not aligned with your values. That means not only leaving a hole with your physical absence but a hole with your spiritual absence as well. Don't make that mistake. When we don't use our gifts, we move away from a state of fulfillment and harmony. We each have a responsibility to identify and utilize our talents to positively impact this world and the people who matter to us. You have a purpose, and it's up to you to make that purpose a reality.

"I don't need a financial advisor — I can handle my wealth management on my own."

I get it. You're a self-starter, a go-getter. You don't need anyone holding your hand, and you sure as hell don't need anyone telling you what to do with your money. I agree with you. Here's the thing: A great advisor won't do that. A great advisor recognizes that your money is your money, and what you do with it is entirely your decision.

Now, I know what you're thinking, "Sanger, isn't that what a wealth advisor is for? To tell people what to do with their money?" And to that, I say, "Not at all." A great advisor is there to guide you and provide expert advice, but the decisions are yours. The right advisor will collaborate with you to create a personalized plan that aligns with your values, ensuring you have all the information and resources to make sound decisions.

We all have blind spots. We all have biases and tendencies that can lead us down wrong paths. The right advisor for you will bring a fresh perspective with a trained eye for identifying and addressing those blind spots. Advisors are there to ensure you're not shooting yourself in the foot without even realizing it. That ability only comes from the wisdom gained by leading hundreds, or even thousands, of people along their wealth journey. An experienced advisor with the right approach to the craft has wisdom and insight you won't find on Google.

Think of it this way: would you try to fix your car engine without consulting a mechanic? You can probably figure out how everything works if you research and practice enough, but a lot can go wrong with one simple mistake. The stakes are even higher with your wealth. You could possibly manage most of it on your own, but why expose yourself to unnecessary risks when you have access to an expert on your side?

Don't sell yourself short. You're capable of remarkable things, but you don't have to go at it alone. The right advisor will handle the grunt work so you can reinvest your time in the people and things you value most.

"Wealth management shouldn't cost so much."

Price is only an issue when the value returned doesn't measure up. A **high-value service** can easily make your investment worth it. I believe top-tier expert management is the only option for transforming wealth to significance. An advisor focused on multi-plying your impact is well worth the investment when you see what you can accomplish through that partnership. Think of it like this: If you hire someone specifically to help you save money on taxes, increase your net worth, and save time in the process, how hard would it be to determine after a year if it was worth the spend?

Advice in an area of life with such high stakes shouldn't be cheap when the impact is enormous and the costs of doing it wrong are devastating.

REMOVING YOUR VALUES LEAVES A HOLE YOU CANNOT DIG OUT OF

Early in my career, when I was an inexperienced advisor, I worked with Gerard. Gerard was a rugged man who liked to go at it alone. Partly due to my lack of wisdom and partly because of his impenetrable demeanor, we kept our conversations strict-ly to the status of his portfolio. Nevertheless, we met regularly and talked more often than most of my clients, mainly because Gerard, despite his stoic attitude, loved to talk about the mar-kets and glean any insight he could from me.

Although we didn't have a deep relationship, I thought Gerard was among the clients who valued my work the most.

Until he quit his job.

During one of our regularly scheduled quarterly meetings, Gerard opened the conversation with a surprise announcement. "I quit my job yesterday," he said matter-of-factly, as if he was reporting the details of his lunch that afternoon.

"Wow, that's a big change," I responded, wide-eyed. We hadn't discussed this before.

"Yeah, I figure I'm going to start my own business. I was getting tired of working with those people."

At that moment, I, on the one hand, wished Gerard had involved me in the decision-making process leading up to this big life event, but on the other, I was extraordinarily happy for him. He had so many possibilities at his fingertips, and I knew his new business would be successful no matter what. He was a sharp guy. And to be fair, I couldn't expect to be involved when all we'd ever talked about before was capital markets and the economy.

With his stoic tone, Gerard said, "So I guess I'm going to need to roll that 401(k) over into an IRA so you can manage it. There's about $2 million in there now, I think."

"Sounds good."

I didn't hear anything from Gerard about moving the 401(k) dollars after that meeting. However, I didn't want to be pushy, so after a couple of weeks of silence, I decided to let it wait until our next quarterly meeting, although I wondered what was going on. Gerard was surely focused on starting his business with every ounce of free time imaginable. I was more than slightly worried that this sizable piece of his investment portfolio was not getting its rightful attention.

During the next meeting, we sat down and reviewed the accounts that I was managing. After talking through the numbers, I asked about his other assets to get a clearer picture of his current financial status. First, we looked at how much the house was worth. Then we calculated the value of the ranch. Last, I asked him, "How much is in the 401(k) right now?"

"Hmm... um... let me check." Suddenly Gerard was flustered in a way I'd never seen.

I waited while he pulled out his phone and navigated to find his account balance. He stared at the screen for several breaths. "Um... it's about $1.4 million," he nearly whispered.

The stock market was down about 10 percent from when we last met. The accounts I was managing were only down 5 percent. Gerard's 401(k) was down 30 percent. How does that even happen? I pulled up my notes from last time to double-check and make sure I remembered correctly. Gerard's 401(k) had dropped 30 percent when his other assets were only down single digits. Before I could even formulate a response to this news, Gerard scrambled to justify his situation. "But that was all in oil stocks. I'm out of those now, don't worry." Just when I thought things couldn't get worse.

I realized Gerard had ratcheted up the risk inside his account without first asking me for any insight or advice, got immediately punished for his aggressive posture, then sold out of everything at the bottom. I was heartbroken for him. This stress was exactly the opposite of the mindset he needed while starting his business.

Gerard never moved the 401(k) to me to manage for him. Instead, he kept trying to win back his losses for the next several years through aggressive bets and failed attempts to time the market. Part of me wanted to scoff and act indignant. "If only he had asked me for my advice first! I did so well with his other accounts. I could have done the same thing with his 401(k) and avoided those huge losses for him."

What I realized quickly was that I was the failure here. I had failed Gerard. By confining our conversations exclusively to market performance, I kept Gerard from uncovering what truly mattered. Worse yet, I didn't know what mattered to him, either. If I had done my job correctly, I wouldn't have been surprised by his business start-up. If I had spent the time to get to know Gerard beyond his portfolio, I would have rightly gained the trust necessary for him to feel comfortable talking through these big decisions. Gerard kept these big decisions out of our relationship, not because he wasn't smart, but because I didn't do a good enough job showing him I cared.

To get the right advice, you must be comfortable being vulnerable. You must be okay with asking what might seem like silly questions. The right advisor will make this easy for you and ensure that avoidable mistakes don't happen.

I wasn't born with an innate ability to guide others toward great financial decisions. The wisdom and knowledge I have now, after over a decade of experience, did not magically transfer to me from my father, either. I learned how to help people like Gerard by seeing firsthand the consequences of not talking about what truly matters. Failing to incorporate our values and our noble aims into our financial decision-making from the get-go leaves us to blindly follow the whims of our emotions, daily market movements, and narrowly focused tips from friends.

It is next to impossible to consistently make the best decision for you when you do not make a conscious, diligent effort to bring truth to the forefront of each choice you make with your dollars. That truth is the truth of your values.

1 CORINTHIANS 10:12

CHAPTER 8

Some Advice on *Taking Advice*

"Advice is like mushrooms.
The wrong kind can prove fatal."
— Charles E. McKenzie

A relationship with the right advisor can improve your net investment return (after fees) by up to 3 percent when compared to what your returns would be with you directing your investment portfolio without advice.[6] This isn't a number I made up willy-nilly. It comes from Vanguard, an investment company founded in 1975 and known for making low-cost index funds available to the average retail investor. The entire basis for their founding was that the investment world was unnecessarily expensive, to the detriment of average Americans.

Vanguard was one of the earliest providers of self-directed investment accounts, which allow you to be your own advisor and control your investments with little to no costs.

Logic would say they have a built-in bias *against* paying for advice. Yet, in their research paper "Putting a value on your value: Quantifying Advisor's Alpha," they found through implementing select strategies, advisors can improve clients' returns significantly — up to or even exceeding 3 percent. The strategies they claim make a difference are:

- Suitable asset allocation using broadly diversified funds/ETFs
- Cost-effective implementation (expense ratios)
- Rebalancing
- Behavioral coaching
- Asset location
- Spending strategy (withdrawal order)
- Total return versus income investing

When looking for the right advice for something, we commonly ask people closest to us for guidance. After all, your friends and family are the people you trust and care about the most.

However, even the smartest and most well-intentioned people in our lives likely don't have the same level of expertise and experience as an expert who spends all day, every day, delving deeply into those specific issues.

As an advisor, I know firsthand that actual knowledge and expertise are crucial for giving good advice.

You may think that since the people closest to you know your personality better than anyone else, they have expertise. Ok — but do you share your household budget with them? Do they know your net worth? Do they know your risk profile in your investment account? More important than anything else, have you explicitly shared your core values and financial aspirations with them?

Even an intelligent money manager can easily give the wrong advice without all this crucial information. Uncle Doug, who works in marketing, has hardly a prayer of giving you the right financial advice without it.

So, while it's natural to turn to those closest to us for guidance, it's essential to consider the source. Has this person been here before? Have they led others to where you want to go? Do they truly know what matters to you?

It's not only a question of emotionally based trust but also a question of expertise, knowledge, and wisdom.

When I first started training for my Ironman triathlons, I searched everywhere on the internet for advice. Unfortunately, good advice was hard to find. Sometimes I would watch a thirty-minute YouTube video only to discover the tips didn't apply because I didn't have access to specific training equipment. Sometimes I would read articles full of information and realize that implementing the advice was not practical for my lifestyle. More than a few times, I took advice that didn't work for me based on my body type or training style.

Seemingly half of the information I found directly conflicted with the other information I found. Some people said foam rolling was essential; others said it was pointless. Some folks said certain nutrition bars worked best, while others assured they were essentially poison.

The most convincing advice always came from friends or people I knew personally. It was convincing because I trusted them deeply as humans. I should not, however, have trusted them as triathlon coaches. The advice I got from people in my life often turned out to be the worst. I can't blame my friends, either. They didn't know any information about me or my goals that would make them qualified to give the right advice. Some of them had been there before and completed full-distance triathlons, but none had done what I set out to do with such a short recovery period. Indeed, none of them had ever led another person across the finish line.

Eventually, I looked in the mirror and realized I needed to follow my advice to get advice. That meant getting a trained advisor. Or, in this case, a triathlon coach. Jerrett Gordon and I met regularly throughout my training over Zoom to build out a training plan unique to my specific goal — complete two Ironman triathlons in three weeks.

When I hired Jerrett, a weight immediately lifted off my shoulders. I no longer needed to spend hours searching for the answers on YouTube or Reddit threads. Instead, I knew I had someone I could count on. Jerrett knew who I was and what motivated me. He knew where I was — an inexperienced athlete who had not competitively raced in any of the three triathlon disciplines since summer swim team at the community pool in elementary school. He understood the challenges of preparing me in time to finish two full-distance triathlons within a month of each other. And as an experienced coach with many other successful triathletes under his guidance, he knew how to get me there.

He acted as a centralized source of advice, allowing me to cut out all the other noise in my life.

You might face the same problem in your financial life — an overabundance of information online, tips and tricks that don't work, and overenthusiastic friends who give unsolicited advice without the ability to see the bigger picture.

GETTING ADVICE FROM A DJ – WHEN FRIENDS DON'T KNOW THE WHOLE STORY

An advisor friend of mine, who I will keep anonymous, told me a cautionary tale of his experience working with one of his very first clients when he started as a financial advisor in the nineties. He worked for a young woman who had started her career working behind the scenes of a morning radio show. The show was top-rated locally and nationally. For years, the show was number one for morning FM radio.

For anonymity, we'll call the woman Kendra and her co-host Rip.

Kendra had all the appearances of financial success. Yes, she worked behind the scenes, but she was part of an incredibly successful team. However, Rip was making a killing, while Kendra was merely getting by in terms of salary. In meeting with her advisor, Kendra's main focus was getting out of debt and budgeting so she could start saving. She had some money in an IRA, but she would need to ratchet up the savings fairly aggressively unless she wanted her plan to be to pray for a bigger contract one day and hope the show never got canceled.

Rip cared for Kendra. And he meant well. He was incredibly open about what he was doing financially and never hesitated to let Kendra in on the conversations. He'd often recommend she invest in risky stocks or real estate ventures without considering her current debt — because he didn't know about it.

After years of listening to Rip tell her what she should do with her money, despite his lack of understanding of her situation, Kendra eventually gave in. She pulled all the money out of her account and took out a second mortgage on her home to invest in an illiquid private real estate investment. The investment provided no guarantee that Kendra could sell if she needed the money.

With Rip's risk-seeking voice in her ear, Kendra went all in on the radio show, banking her entire financial security on a new contract hopefully coming one day.

Sadly, the worst-case scenario for both Rip and Kendra played out. Rip tragically and suddenly died due to medical complications that were detected too late. At the snap of a finger, the radio show was over. Well-meaning but nonetheless flawed advice left Kendra in an unrecoverable hole. She now had two mortgages and no job. To make matters worse, the private real estate investment underperformed dramatically. As a result, Kendra's net worth went from positive to negative overnight.

TEN QUESTIONS TO ASK ANY ADVISOR

What are your qualifications and experience?

You should understand the advisor's background, education, and professional experience. Whether you are racing a triathlon, selling your business, or building your financial future, you want someone on your side who has been down the path before and guided others to where you hope to be. They need to take the burden of finding all the answers off your shoulders, just as my triathlon coach, Jerrett, did for me. You can focus on your life without the fear that you're missing something important.

How do you make your money?

Before doing business with an advisor, you should know how they pay their bills. Are they fee-only or commission-based? Do they charge for advice directly, or are they only paid for asset management? How an advisor gets paid should directly correspond with the value they deliver and align with the value you seek. Knowing this can help you understand any potential conflicts of interest and judge whether the advisor just wants more sales or wants to provide the best advice tailored to you.

What is your investment philosophy?

Many advisors don't have one. Great advisors do. You want someone with a philosophy that works, that makes sense to you, and that you like. If it doesn't meet all three criteria, keep looking.

What are your fees?

Simple. What does it cost to work with this person, and can they justify that expense with the value they will provide?

What is your process for developing a financial plan?

A great advisor will customize your financial plan uniquely to your values and aspirations, but they also will have a process for how to get there. It should be simple to articulate and related to what you hope to achieve.

What is your process for monitoring and reviewing my investments?

This is a question most folks don't think to ask. Many advisors will get thrown off at that moment, realizing they don't have one. A great advisor won't miss a beat when answering.

How will you communicate with me?

Does your advisor send annual email updates or call you personally each month? You should want to know from the jump when, how, and if they proactively communicate.

Can you provide references from current clients?

To protect confidentiality, a great advisor would give you the name and contact information of a family he works for only with their explicit approval. Still, a great advisor who does excellent work will have at least one enthusiastic advocate eager to share the good news.

What happens if I'm not satisfied?

As you might imagine, great advisors don't face this problem often. But you ought to understand what level of commitment is being asked of you and what your options are if you want to end the relationship.

Which other advisors and companies are your partners?

Even independent advisors have companies they partner with and professional advisors in other fields they rely on. You can judge a lot about an advisor by the company they keep.

PROVERBS 15:31-32

CHAPTER 9

Overwhelmed: Too Much *Wealth,* Too Many *Options*

"Of all the liars in the world, sometimes the worst are our own fears." – Rudyard Kipling

THE RICH MAN WHO ACTED POOR

One of my clients, Randy, didn't come from money. He grew up in rural Missouri. And you could tell by the way he pronounced it, "Mizzurrah." His family never had money. His father was a silversmith who made tools for the local corn and soybean farmers. His mother hand-sewed all the clothes for him and his three sisters. They were indeed "dirt floor poor" in that the floor of their 1940s farmhouse was made out of polished dirt.

Randy moved to Texas after high school and worked for a local government weapons contractor in Fort Worth. He saved money diligently and never spent a dime on anything he didn't absolutely need. As a result, he retired with more money than he could have ever imagined. With $10 million in investments, he could have done anything he wanted with his life when he retired at 65.

Randy, though, never saw himself as wealthy. He always feared that he didn't have enough. It didn't require a genius to calculate that Randy would never spend his $10 million. He lived in a low-rent apartment on the sketchy side of town, drove a twenty-year-old beat-up Honda Accord, never traveled outside the state, and never went out on weekends. He cooked every meal at home, only going out once a month — twice if there was a holiday.

Randy's only hobby was researching his family history on-line, which didn't require any expenses.

When asked why he didn't spend his money, he always responded with a version of, "I want to make sure I have enough." Enough for what? The answer was never clear.

When Randy's advisor told him Randy was one of the top 1% of Americans by net worth, Randy rejected the facts. He said, "No way, I'm not some rich guy."

Randy couldn't allow himself to think he was rich. His relationship with his wealth suffered because of scars from his childhood. He remembered the "rich" men in suits who auctioned off his family home on the courthouse steps when his father stopped making payments. A laceration on his hand from one of his machines forced him to give up silversmithing when Randy was still in school, leaving the family with no source of income.

Randy remembered being poor. Vividly. His identity was rooted in his humble beginnings. In his mind, being rich meant being everything opposite of where he came from. To be rich was to be one of those people who gentrified the small town he grew up in, displacing families like his own in favor of the expansion of factory farming.

Randy's fear of wealth was a heavy fur coat in the summertime, weighing him down and suffocating him at every turn, preventing him from enjoying the fruits of his labor.

He couldn't hide the symptoms, either. The depression, the anxiety, and the stress that accompanied the fear followed Randy everywhere he went. Eventually, those ails won the battle. Randy fell ill at age 73 and spent his last years in a long-term care facility. He never did make a distribution from his investment portfolio or find anything to spend his money on. He never transformed wealth to significance. He was too consumed by fear.

Fear of wealth: It's real.

It may seem odd. How are people who hire a wealth advisor afraid of being wealthy? Aren't they already wealthy? The answer is yes; they are already wealthy. Virtually everyone who has a fear of wealth is.

Poor people are not afraid of wealth. I mean, truly poor people are not afraid of wealth. No child in Africa walking ten miles round trip to bring clean water to his sick mother back in the village, battling disease-ridden mosquitos, is afraid of money. No, this is a uniquely privileged problem to face. And it's one you may be facing, knowingly or not. Yes, it is true some poor people manage to stay poor due to unwise money decisions stemming from an unhealthy relationship or mindset toward money. I am not talking about them. I am talking specifically about people who have money yet are afraid of the wealth that money may provide. One cannot be afraid of wealth if one does not have the means to obtain it, I would argue. It's akin to being afraid of the dark while living on the Sun. If one has never known darkness and never will, can one truly be afraid?

THE SCIENCE OF FEAR

When we experience fear, the amygdala, a small almond-shaped structure in the brain's temporal lobe, signals the hypothalamus, which activates the sympathetic nervous system.[7] This causes the release of adrenaline and other stress hormones, leading to the fight-or-flight response.[8] This response causes changes in the body, such as increased heart rate, blood pressure, and muscle tension. Additionally, the prefrontal cortex, responsible for reasoning and decision-making, may shut down, causing an inability to think clearly or make rational choices, leading to a possible third response — freezing.

This response — known by scientists as "tonic immobility"[9] — is an adaptive mechanism that evolved to help animals avoid detection by predators or other threats. For example, when an animal, such as an opossum, experiences freezing, the body enters a state of heightened arousal. Instead of responding with fight or flight, the animal remains motionless and unresponsive. This looks like a form of "playing dead," as it can make the predator lose interest in the prey. It also conserves energy, reducing the animal's movement and noise, which could attract predator attention.

In humans, the freeze response can become chronic and last for extended periods, sometimes even years. This can happen due to prolonged exposure to emotional trauma or stressful situations or as a result of unresolved traumatic experiences in the past.

Being in a chronic freeze state[10] can affect an individual's ability to function in daily life. They may experience symptoms such as difficulty with emotional regulation, difficulty with social interactions, and a general sense of detachment from the present moment. They may also have trouble with trust and intimacy and may feel a sense of isolation or hopelessness.

When we're afraid, our brains often go into freeze mode — we stall, pause, or do nothing at all. And that's exactly what happens with money decisions, too. When we get scared about finances and freeze up, we don't make decisions about our wealth. We avoid decisions about saving, investing, spending, and planning. We don't react; we simply do nothing at all and hope the monster doesn't see us as long as we stand really, really still.

FEAR OF WEALTH

Money for money's sake is not the end goal. In the same vein, success for the sake of success is not the end goal either. Yet, success is necessary to reach significance through wealth. Simply put, we cannot transform wealth to significance without first attaining financial success. I spoke earlier in the book about how the journey toward success is unfulfilling. Some people suffer from a fear of wealth that prevents them from ever achieving the success first necessary to act as the building block toward significance.

The fear of success, also known as achievement anxiety or success phobia, is a sneaky little bug creeping up on us when we least expect it. It's that nagging doubt that once we achieve our goals, we'll be unable to handle the responsibilities that come with the achievement, or worse, we'll lose something we value in the process.

Let's be real: The fear of wealth is not only about the destination; it is also about the journey. We fear the uncertainty of how others and ourselves will treat us when we have money. We become anxious about change and the unknown. Fear of success is always lurking in the shadows, the evil twin of the fear of failure.

Sometimes the fear of wealth is glaringly obvious. Other times it's a subtle undercurrent disguised in patterns of thoughts and actions. It requires a healthy dose of self-awareness to recognize this fear and how to conquer it.

Often, this fear comes from the fear of responsibility or from feelings of inadequacy. Individuals may feel that they are incapable of handling the responsibilities that come with wealth, or they worry they won't live up to the expectations of others. As a result, they may feel they do not deserve wealth and will be exposed as frauds or imposters if they achieve it.

If you hold negative beliefs about yourself and your abilities, such as feeling not good enough, not smart enough, or not talented enough, these beliefs can cause you to fear that you cannot manage the challenges that come with wealth.

HOW FEAR OF WEALTH MANIFESTS

One day in college, after working on the cattle ranch, my fellow ranch hands and I had a bonfire. I was the youngest by far. The oldest hand, Dean, was forty-seven. We hung out at his house, a single-wide trailer home that was falling apart before our eyes.

Each of us made $8 an hour, including Dean. The rest of us were young, so Dean seized the opportunity to give unsolicited life advice. What he said that night always stuck with me.

"I never did want to be rich," he said.

Looking around at his crumbling trailer, I thought he had succeeded in reaching that non-goal. It was a non-goal in the sense that his aim was not to achieve but to avoid. He didn't want to have something; instead, he wanted to ensure he did not have something.

Fear of wealth looks different in various aspects of life. These are some ways it shows its ugly head.

Avoidance

Like Randy, some people choose to avoid facing the reality of the financial success they have already reached. They refute the idea that they are wealthy. A friend of mine has a successful car dealership. He has $100 million in investments, not including the value of his primary business. Yet even he refuses to call himself rich.

Procrastination

You are avoiding beginning the financial planning process. There are things you know you ought to do — start saving, start investing, start planning, start consulting with a specialized tax attorney, start engaging a business consultant, and start working with a wealth advisor. But you avoid doing whatever you need to do to move to the next level — to avoid staying on your plateau — while comforting yourself with the lie, "Someday I will...."

Perfectionism

By keeping an impossible standard of perfection, disappointment is inevitable. These people are never satisfied with how much they earn, save, invest, or grow their portfolios. A friend of mine made $90,000 per year as an engineer and managed to save over half of his earnings after taxes. Yet, he often told me he thought he wasn't saving enough. But what is "enough"? The perfectionist will move the goalposts to keep his standard of wealth always a hair out of reach.

Self-sabotage

This happens in different ways. One typical method is doing what Dean did — avoid success altogether and tell himself that's what he wanted. If he sought wealth, he might have failed and then would have had to acknowledge his lack of success. It was much easier to create the narrative that living paycheck to paycheck for mere pennies in poverty, working eighty hours a week of manual labor, was precisely the life he'd dreamed of or had chosen. But was it? And if so, why? He'd sabotaged himself by having no goal — or an anti-goal.

Another way people sabotage their goals is through compulsive and erratic spending behaviors. Some people have everything going for them financially but make one wrong decision that derails their plan. The biggest culprit of this is buying a house that is too expensive. The home-buying process is long, so purchasing on a whim is difficult, although not impossible. Yet, people will derail their plans by taking on significant debt that hamstrings their cash flow. It works as a perfectly terrible solution to facing their fears. If you add a considerable expense to your monthly budget, you cannot save at the rate you should. Failure now becomes inevitable, and you've actively chosen it.

Lack of Motivation

Randy exhibited this in spades. People afraid of financial success can never seem to think of anything worth spending their money on. They cannot set financial objectives because they need more motivation to dream of what is possible. They need the motivation of a noble aim — a Significance Plan.

CAUSES OF FEAR OF WEALTH

As we are each unique, the fear of wealth has a variety of potential causes. Often, people are at least partly unaware of how some of these things influence them until they deal with the reasons. Negative self-talk can reinforce the belief that we cannot or should not have wealth for ourselves.

"Wealth causes pain."

We carry with us the influence of our childhood environment and, sometimes, spend a lifetime healing the wounds. For example, if you grew up in a household whose members consistently disparaged wealth, you may unconsciously fear becoming wealthy yourself. Think back to your earliest money memory. Be detailed and write it all out — everything you thought, felt, saw, and experienced. Who was there? What did they say? If your parents or primary caregivers had a poverty mindset, and they expressed that openly in your presence, you might have an unconsciously negative view of money.

If your parents struggled to make ends meet when you were growing up, you might have developed a mindset that money is scarce and that it is impossible to have enough of it. Witnessing your parents' stress and frustration because of money problems may have reinforced this belief. As counterintuitive as it may seem, you might develop a fear of becoming wealthy, as wealth represents a source of pain.

"I don't deserve this."

This is incredibly common, particularly for recipients of instant wealth — business owners who suddenly receive a big check after selling their company or folks who inherit wealth from a loved one who has passed. This suddenness can cause some to feel as if their wealth wasn't earned. In the business owner's case, it is blatantly not true. In the beneficiary's situation, it is irrelevant. Both individuals now have wealth and, thus, have a responsibility to be good stewards of that wealth. Guilt will only rob them of their opportunity to create an impact.

"I'm not who they think I am."

Imposter syndrome is related to guilt. It's a phenomenon in which an individual doubts their accomplishments and fears being exposed as a fraud.[11] Even the most successful people have suffered from this illogical thought. Albert Einstein was once reported as saying to a friend, "The exaggerated esteem in which my lifework is held makes me very ill at ease. I feel compelled to think of myself as an involuntary swindler."[12]

This can lead to a fear of becoming wealthy if you feel undeserving of your success and thus worry that others will see you as a fraud when you become wealthy.

For instance, if you have imposter syndrome, you may feel that you've only achieved your success through luck or by fooling others. As a result, you may not believe you can acquire wealth and may fear that you won't be able to keep it. This can lead to a fear of becoming wealthy because you may feel unable to handle the responsibilities that come with it.

Negative self-talk, such as "I'm not good enough" or "I don't deserve this," can reinforce this fear.

"If I have wealth, people won't like me anymore."

Or, worse, they'll only like you for your money. The fear that our community, or people in our lives, may react negatively to our wealth is common for people who maintain relationships with those with a scarcity mindset. You may unconsciously be afraid of how your friends and family will treat you if they are not wealthy, but you are.

"I can't be trusted with wealth; I might make a terrible mistake and lose everything."

If you had money before and had a negative experience, you might still let that wretched past cloud your judgment. Maybe you once had money and lost it on a bad investment. Maybe you mismanaged your spending years ago and are afraid of trusting yourself in that same situation in the future. Or maybe you saw this happen to your parents and fear it will happen to you.

Many imagine a future where they have substantial wealth and manage it poorly. The fear of blowing their opportunity leads to a fear of having the opportunity itself.

"Money complicates everything. I don't want to deal with that."

Alternatively, a person may be afraid that having money will make life more complicated, which, in some ways, is true. There are unique problems that wealth presents. The good news is that these problems are a responsibility rather than a lack of freedom.

ARE YOU WILLING TO SACRIFICE YOUR NOBLE GOALS?

Simply put, you will never reach your highest, noblest aim without conquering the fear of wealth. The fear of wealth will inhibit your transformation of the dollars you have at your disposal to a lasting impact. It will rob you of a future where you transform wealth to significance.

Conquer Your Fear

Living in a constant state of anxiety will have a lot of long-term negative ramifications for you and those you want to do something for. Don't let the fear of wealth or failure hold you back from the impact you were born to create. So, it's time to deal with your emotions more healthily. Here are some suggestions:

- **Journal** – What is your vision of a wealthy life? What would you do if you had all the money in the world?

Imagine this scenario; you're standing on your front porch. In your hands are two leather suitcases. You can smell the leather. They're heavy. They're heavy because each one is full of cash. Now, where are you going? The answer to this question will show you what your limited mindset is currently causing you to sacrifice. Here's a helpful format for composing your thoughts.

Date: _____

Today's Money Mood: (circle one)
Mad, Sad, Glad, Afraid, Ashamed

1. **Reflection:** Spend a few minutes reflecting on your thoughts and feelings about money. Write down any specific situations or experiences that come to mind — free flow for a few minutes.

2. **Gratitude:** Write down three things you are grateful for related to money or your financial situation. This could be as basic as having a job, having a roof over your head, or having access to food and water.

3. **Fear:** Write down any fears or anxieties about money. This could be fear of not having enough, losing what you have, or not being able to provide for yourself or your family.

4. **Purpose:** Think about your noble aim and the purpose of your money. What do you want to accomplish with your money? How can aligning your wealth with your purpose provide you with motivation and fulfillment?

5. **Action:** Write down one action for the day that will move you toward your financial objectives. This

could be as simple as creating a budget, starting a savings plan, or seeking advice from your advisor.

6. **Closing Thoughts:** Write down your last thoughts and insights about your relationship with money. How do you feel after reflecting on your emotions and creating an action plan? What future steps will cultivate a healthy relationship with your money?

- **Reflect** – Sit with your thoughts. Meditate and resist the urge to say something. My grandpa, Joe Guy, an accomplished artist, was quoted as saying, "Better to be an anonymous thing than to be about saying something, for the saying of something, in its calculating, conceals. Meditating one thing clears the way for the unsaid."[13] The source and depth of your fears may not be immediately apparent to you. Even the most extraordinarily self-aware person is highly unlikely to discover, with clarity, such complex inhibitions without deep contemplation. Creating moments of *nothing* allows space for the *something* of the most profound truth within you to speak.

- **Acknowledge** – Once you have found your fear, acknowledge it. By writing down your fear, you bring it to the center of your attention and can dismantle it consciously rather than allowing it to dictate your choices subconsciously.

- **Explore** – It's time for a trip down memory lane and to reflect on your experiences. Was it something that happened in your childhood or adulthood that's holding you back from reaching your goals? What message did you glean from those experiences, and how is it affecting your vision of a life of wealth? Most importantly, what would your life look like if you never chased after this idea of success?

Give yourself the freedom to dig deep and review your journal every week. By identifying patterns and themes related to success in your thoughts and behaviors, you can counteract them. Once you've identified your negative beliefs and self-talk, it's time to reframe them into something positive and empowering.

IS THAT FEELING REALLY FEAR?

You may feel something — but is it actually fear? Or maybe a better question is, does it have to stay fear?

People often misinterpret excitement as anxiety. Harvard Business School professor Alison Wood Brooks conducted research showing that shifting from anxiety to calm is extraordinarily difficult and counterproductive.[14] Both anxiety and excitement are what psychologists commonly refer to as "arousal emotions." The substantive difference between anxiety and excitement is the story we tell ourselves about those feelings. In Brooks' research, she refers to the shift from anxiety to excitement as "anxiety reappraisal."

It's possible that your perceived anxiety surrounding wealth is actually the excitement of imagining its possibilities and impact.

Even if you are anxious, you can reframe your negative feelings of fear and anxiety to positive ones of excitement and anticipation before you let fear dictate your future.

Once you choose a noble aim of significance, these fears will subside much more easily. The fear of wealth is not a concern if the motivation is the service of others. The fear of failure is less prominent if your work has a purpose beyond self-serving.

Here's how focusing on significance versus worst-case scenarios can help you relieve your fear:

- Achieving significance in life is a more empowering and uplifting aim than simply avoiding disaster.
- When you focus on what you want to achieve vs. what you want to avoid, you become more confident, which can reduce fear and anxiety.
- When you focus on what you're aiming toward, you are less likely to get bogged down in doomsday thinking, and you're more likely to find creative solutions to big problems.
- Focusing on significance helps you see challenges as opportunities for growth and learning rather than as threats to be avoided.
- When you focus on creating impact and making a difference, fear is less likely to stop you.
- By focusing on significance, you can cultivate a sense of purpose and meaning in your life.
- By shifting your focus from worst-case scenarios to significance, you gain control of your life and create a future you're excited about.

PSALM 61:2

CHAPTER 10

What Does True *Significance* Mean to You?

"A legacy is not what's left tomorrow when you're gone. It's what you give, create, impact, and contribute today while you're here that then happens to live on." – Rasheed Ogunlaru

M oney is a tool, a means to an end. We can use it to fix, build, and move things and to make things happen. But like any tool, using it is not the end goal. The end goal is what you use the tool for — what you build, fix, move, and make happen. And, to live a purposeful life, the end goal ought to be significant.

Yet, significance means something different to each person. You've thought about your values and what's important to you. Now it's time to see what aligning your wealth with your values might achieve. What does true significance mean to you?

MAKING A POSITIVE IMPACT

When you use your money to do something significant, you make a difference in the world. You're doing something that matters, something that will have an impact. Whether donating to a charity that aligns with your values or starting a business that serves a need in your community, you're using your wealth to make the world a better place.

Simon Sinek, author of *Start with Why*,[15] believes that creating impact starts with having a clear sense of purpose and understanding the "why" behind what you do. He argues that people are naturally drawn to those who have a clear sense of purpose and that by focusing on our why, we can inspire others to join us in our mission. He encourages leaders to focus on the collective good and make decisions that will benefit themselves, the people they lead, and the communities they serve.

If a company is clear on its why, then what they sell and how they make money become somewhat irrelevant, Sinek says. A company can easily change what it sells if it learns that doing so will better serve the why — the mission.

If you are crystal clear on the why behind your money, what you should do with it will become clear, too. If you attempt to operate without a why you will forever be stuck in an endless loop of concern regarding the "what." Should I invest in foreign stocks? Should I buy an annuity? Should I be putting more money into my retirement account?

In my experience as a professional, the folks who worry most about the "what" with their money are the ones who have no clear "why" for their wealth.

Choose Your Risk

American businessman Jim Rohn cleverly said, "I'll tell you how risky life is. You're not going to get out alive. That's risky."

His point was that everything involves risk. Unfortunately, there is no risk-free money solution. In the financial world, we refer to risk-free investments as those with guaranteed returns and virtually no possibility that they will drop in value or become worthless. This path may sound like it has no risk, yet there are risks, to be sure. With guaranteed returns, the risk is that the return may not keep pace with inflation over time or that alternative investment strategies may have provided a better return over that period. There are often liquidity risks with such guaranteed-return investments, meaning there is a risk that you cannot get your money when you need it.

That is not to say you should avoid any investment labeled "risk-free." On the contrary, you must decide which risks are worth taking and which will move you closer, more gracefully, toward your unique aim of significance.

Being too risk-averse can prevent you from making meaningful investments or donations that have a significant impact.

Think Long Term

Impact does not happen overnight. Being too focused on short-term gains will create anxiety and cause you to lose focus on your aim. If you are dedicated to a plan with your wealth that will generate a positive impact for your family and your community, yet you're still focused on daily, weekly, or even monthly returns, what you are doing is akin to taking a road trip to the Grand Canyon, sticking your neck out the car window, and watching how fast the asphalt moves by. You're missing the point entirely.

Creatively solve for the needs of others

Charitable giving can undoubtedly create an impact. But it is not the only way. Think about the needs of others in your life and how you can use your money to serve them. Be open to new ideas and perspectives on finding innovative ways to create impact.

Impact investing might be a part of your Significance Plan, too. Impact investments are investments made with the intended outcome of generating measurable social good alongside a financial return.

FULFILLING YOUR VALUES

Money can buy you many things, but it can't buy you fulfillment. That comes from using your wealth purposefully to create something meaningful that makes you feel you've made a difference. When you make a difference in the world, you're not only helping others; you're helping yourself too.

Brené Brown, a researcher and author, writes about the importance of fulfillment in her work on vulnerability, shame, and courage. She argues that fulfillment comes from living a life that is true to oneself and that this requires the courage to be vulnerable and to let go of the need for perfection and external validation. In her book *Daring Greatly*,[16] she writes about how fulfillment is not about achieving success or happiness but about living a life of purpose and meaning. She argues that true fulfillment comes from engaging in activities and relationships that align with our values and passions. This requires the willingness to be vulnerable and accept risks.

If you apply your dollars toward the things, experiences, and causes that align with you, you will move closer to fulfillment. Unfortunately, no investment will magically make you feel at peace with your money. There is not one financial decision you can make that will quell your worries. To find fulfillment, you must choose to save, invest, and spend your money on what brings the most authenticity to your life.

LEAVING AN AMAZING FAMILY LEGACY

We all want to leave a mark on the world — to be remembered for something. Even if you don't think so. According to psychologist Abraham Maslow's hierarchy of needs, the desire for self-actualization and to reach one's full potential is a human need at the top of the pyramid.[17] This includes the desire to make a difference and leave a lasting impact on the world. Even people who may not actively consider leaving a legacy still have an innate desire to contribute somehow to society and be remembered. To strive to leave a mark is fundamental to being human.

Maslow argues that if you have fulfilled the other basic needs — physiological and safety needs — you are freer to focus on self-actualization, self-transcendence, and leaving a legacy. My call to you is that by you reading this book right now, you are in such a position. You — yes, you — are wealthier than your ancestors could have dreamed. You are wealthier than a large swath of humanity, and you don't need a mansion to prove it.

You have the extraordinary luxury of being able to leave a legacy with your money. This is the most exciting opportunity of your life.

Legacy is the impact you leave behind after your time on Earth is finished. You will leave one, whether you like it or not. But, without planning, it will be like my grandfather — smaller, less thoughtful, and less positive than it could have been, which we discussed in Chapter 2. With planning, you can be like Oliver and transform your family's relationship with wealth.

Tim Ferriss, author of *The 4-Hour Work Week*,[18] encourages people to think about their legacy, not in terms of traditional markers such as wealth or fame, but in terms of the impact they have on the world and the people around them. He suggests people should focus on creating a positive impact in the areas they are most passionate about and be intentional in their actions and decisions to make a lasting impact. He also emphasizes the importance of mentorship and passing on knowledge and skills to future generations to leave a legacy.

Spend the time and do the work to know clearly what legacy you want to leave, then write it down. Finally, create a 100-year plan for your money. When you think about what you want your money to do for the world 100 years from now, what is truly important to you about your legacy will become clear.

When you have your 100-year plan, hold annual family meetings to discuss the legacy you want to leave behind. Do this with your children, grandchildren, and even great-grandchildren if you have them. The best way to ensure the legacy you dream of stays intact after you die is to speak it into existence and do so often. By simply vocalizing your legacy plan, you are giving life and energy to your legacy.

As simple goals do not define or confine your significance, neither do measurable objectives alone constrain your legacy. James Clear, author of the book *Atomic Habits*, highlights this point when he talks about creating a "systems legacy" rather than simply a "results legacy."[19] He suggests that instead of focusing on achieving a specific outcome or goal, we should focus on building systems and habits that will leave a lasting impact. Clear argues that by doing this, we are not only creating a legacy for ourselves but also leaving behind something that will continue to benefit others in the future.

In your financial life, you can do this by clearly communicating your values to your children or beneficiaries. Beyond that, collaborate with the next generation. You don't have to have kids to do this effectively — the next generation can be your siblings, charities, or whoever will become the steward of your wealth after you are gone. As you would not draft up a 100-year, or even 10-year, plan for your business without consulting your most trusted employees, you should not try to enact a legacy plan for your wealth without involving the stakeholders in that legacy.

You must do this to leave the next generation to inherit dollars with clear guidance. If not, they will be in the same position I was in when I bought my dad's business — working blindly, guided only by the behavior they observed in you, not by the values underlying that behavior. In addition, they will be burdened with the curse of working tirelessly toward an aim to which they did not agree.

Think about it. Deeply.

What is the best legacy you can leave your family? What is the best legacy you can leave for your friends? What organizations or groups do you want to provide for? What things do you want to ensure the people you love have when you're gone? What values should they embody to have those things?

FINDING NEW FREEDOM

Imagine knowing exactly which decision to make and what to do every time someone asks you. Imagine no longer being frozen by all your fear and worry that you will do something wrong. You can be in that place.

Foundationally, freedom comes from living a life that aligns with your values and purpose. Once you have created a plan to manage your wealth in alignment with what you want to see happen for the greater good, both in the world and in your relationships, you'll suddenly know what to do. Your goals are clear. You know how to reach them. Even when your goals change, you will learn how to realign to the new dynamic.

When you transform wealth to significance, you're living a life that is true to who you are — one that is *free*. During a homily at Oriole Park at Camden Yards in Baltimore on October 8th, 1995, Pope John Paul II spoke directly to the most freedom-loving people the world has ever known and said, "Every generation of Americans needs to know that freedom consists not in doing what we like, but in having the right to do what we ought."[20]

This concept of freedom means we have the power to make choices that align with our values and beliefs rather than being controlled by external influences or our base desires. This is *true* autonomy. To spend our money primarily on pleasure is not freedom. It is the decision of someone enslaved to comfort. To narrow the focus of our relationship with our money down to what it can buy us tomorrow is not freedom. To make financial decisions based on emotions is not freedom, either.

Often, we make money decisions based entirely on emotions. Even massive decisions like buying a new boat when we haven't saved for our children's college fund, buying a new house when we could spend less money by simply remodeling the kitchen, or buying a fancy new car when the old one is still perfectly fine. Sometimes emotions cause us to make investment choices, too — such as pulling money out of an investment account and socking it away in cash due to fear of a falling market. Or perhaps we allocate far too much to an illiquid, highly risky investment due to optimism and excitement over its potential reward. These choices are not freedom. They are devoid of freedom because they are not guided by the noble aim of significance.

A financial decision-making process spearheaded by a clear Significance Plan is much less prone to the control of our emotions.

In his book *Man's Search for Meaning*, Viktor Frankl argues that true freedom is finding meaning and purpose in life. He writes that "everything can be taken away from a man but one thing: the last of the human freedoms — to choose one's attitude in any given set of circumstances, to choose one's own way."[21]

This is true. Despite the smartest money choices and most rock-solid financial plan, there is no surefire way to guarantee we will always retain that which we hold so tightly. If you don't believe me, ask yourself what good Frankl's bank account did him in Auschwitz.

Similarly, Epictetus, a Greek Stoic philosopher, believed that true freedom comes from understanding and accepting our limitations and circumstances rather than trying to control or change them. He believed that our thoughts and attitudes determine our level of freedom rather than external factors. Epictetus taught that true freedom lies in detaching oneself from one's desires and emotions and instead focusing on living a virtuous and rational life. He believed that by doing so, one could achieve inner peace and freedom from suffering. He also taught that freedom lies in the ability to make choices that align with our values rather than being controlled by our impulses, saying, "Freedom is the only worthy goal in life. It is won by disregarding things that lie beyond our control."[22]

To find freedom with your money, follow a few simple guidelines.

Live Within Your Means

Avoid overspending and keeping up with the Joneses. Consistently spending more than you earn can lead to debt and financial stress, limiting your freedom and narrowing your choices.

Seek Constant Progress

Avoid complacency with your money by regularly reviewing your finances. Set objectives so you can track the progress along your Significance Plan's journey. The goals within your business plan are not the aim of the business plan in its entirety. The same is the case with your money. You don't set financial objectives for the sake of having objectives to accomplish; you set objectives to measure your movement toward your noble aim and to measure your progress toward freedom.

Be Transparent and Open

Whether in your relationship with your significant other or your relationship with your wealth advisor, don't keep secrets. Withholding financial information from your partner or spouse will create mistrust and limit your freedom to make choices as a team.

Keeping secrets from your wealth advisor and not being transparent with your Significance Plan will only rob you of the opportunity to benefit from open and honest feedback, guidance, counsel, and wisdom that could move you closer to what you ought to do.

Identify What You Can Control

You can control a few things regarding your money, and these all relate to the decisions that *you* make: when and how much to save; when, how much, and how often you invest; which investments you pursue; and how and when to spend your money. You cannot control how capital markets perform or the state of the economy. Worrying about things outside your control is the antithesis of freedom.

You're now free to implement your Significance Plan. You have the freedom to pursue your noble aim. You have the freedom to make decisions that align with your values. Other companies will tell you that financial freedom means having enough money to buy whatever you want, go wherever you want, and do whatever you want. Doing whatever you want is not true freedom. Pursuing your noble aim, free to make decisions aligned with your values, is true freedom.

GALATIANS 5:1

CHAPTER 11

Where Do
I *Start?*

"The beginning is the most important part of the work."
– Plato

M any times, when I first work with a family, the question on the front of their minds is, "What is the first step?" Geoff asked me that exact question during our first meeting.

Geoff was a humble, quiet man. I could tell from the onset of our conversation that he was nervous about meeting with me. He said as much. Geoff looked the part of a burly lumberjack but spoke softly and without much confidence. I quickly understood why.

"I kind of feel like I'm having to start over," Geoff told me right out of the gate during our first meeting. "I went through a divorce last year, and now I have full custody of my four sons. Sanger, I just don't know where to start."

He didn't need to say more. Geoff's situation had cut his net worth in half overnight at the age of 40. Now, he alone bore the burden of providing for four teenage boys, financially and emotionally.

"Of course, I want to send the triplets to college. Thankfully, I have a little more time with them than I do with my oldest son."

I nodded. "What else?"

"Well, I don't want to have to work my whole life, either. So being able to retire is something I want to work on."

I nodded again. "What else?"

"I want to experience the world with my sons. They've had a hard time the past year. I don't want to live off ramen noodles just so they can go to college. I want to create memories with them."

"Good. That would be an incredible gift to give them. What else?"

After a pensive pause, Geoff smiled for the first time that morning. "I want to be able to help people when the opportunity comes up. I want to help other people through gifts. That's what God calls us to do."

Unbeknownst to Geoff at the time, he had already identified the purpose and significance of his money. The purpose of his money was to make the lives of others better through small acts of generosity and to instill that virtue in his four sons.

"There," I said. "That is where we start."

Once Geoff had identified what significance meant to him, he had created a purpose for his wealth. He didn't need to have tens of millions in the bank to act it out, either. So, Geoff and I worked through the Decision Lab's 5 Key Decisions and built a plan to allow him and his sons to live out that significant aim of helping other people through gifts.

DECISION 1 – DECIDE WHO YOU ARE.

Geoff decided that he was put on this earth to give generously to others and teach his sons to do the same.

DECISION 2 – DECIDE WHERE YOU ARE.

Geoff had modest room in his budget to allocate to discretionary expenses. He had money he could save, but there was no way he could save adequately for retirement, full college tuition for four kids, annual travel for five people, and still have money to give away. He decided he had $2,000 each month to work with as a starting point.

DECISION 3 – DECIDE WHERE YOU ARE GOING.

Geoff determined that the most significant thing he could do with his wealth was to give back, improve the lives of people in his community, and show his sons firsthand how to do that. Therefore, he prioritized helping others with his money over paying his sons' college tuition. After all, the purpose of education was to teach them something valuable, and what could be more valuable than teaching them to be godly men?

DECISION 4 – DECIDE HOW YOU ARE GOING TO GET THERE.

Of course, Geoff and I constructed a plan to save for his retirement in his 401(k) and how to best use the wealth he had at his disposal. Geoff's most unique decision was to give a minimum amount to *other* people each month. To fully live out his noble aim of helping others through gifts, he wanted to hold himself accountable to do that consistently. We started small. At first, Geoff committed to giving $100 per month away to others through small, impactful gifts.

DECISION 5 – DECIDE WHO MATTERS.

Geoff's sons mattered to him. He was able to have a good relationship with them in large part because of the support he received from his church. Geoff decided the congregation of his local church mattered, too.

Over the years, magic happened. Geoff consistently increased not only his savings but also his gift commitment each year. Year after year, Geoff saved a larger percentage of his income and gave away a larger percentage of his income. He had gone from not knowing what the next step could, would, or should be to a father who transformed wealth to significance so his sons could see what purpose looked like firsthand while they lived in his home.

Geoff's four sons didn't have to sacrifice their education, either. Amazingly, each of the four boys attended and graduated college without taking on any debt. They got there through a combination of scholarships and anonymous grants from members of their church. As Geoff had committed to improving the lives of others within his means, he had unknowingly inspired others in his church to do the same for his own family.

The answer to the question, "Where do I start?" does not lie in savings plans, investment strategies, or budgeting tools. The starting line in the journey of transforming wealth to significance is — as outlined in the Decision Lab — to *decide who you are*. Only once you have decided who you are can you articulate what significance means *to you*. It may be bigger or smaller than what significance meant to Geoff and his boys. The size and scope of your aim will depend on your financial capacity, to be sure. Once you make the declarative choice of an aim, magic happens. The next steps become obvious. You can more easily filter out strategies, ideas, and tactics that don't further your aim. Staying motivated gets easier, too. Consistent discipline in any healthy behavior — like dieting or saving money — isn't always easy. Remaining committed in challenging times becomes much easier when you have a calling bigger than yourself.

A CLEAR FIRST STEP

Embarking upon a lifelong journey of transforming wealth to significance requires years of commitment. Motivation makes years of commitment much easier. A clear, compelling purpose or meaning in life provides the only sustaining motivation.

Daniel Pink is a best-selling author and a leading voice in the intersection of work, motivation, and behavioral science. In his book *Drive: The Surprising Truth About What Motivates Us*, Pink argues that purpose-driven motivation is a critical factor in driving creativity, productivity, and work satisfaction. Pink claims that the traditional model of motivation, which is based on rewards and punishments, does not sufficiently motivate people. Instead, he argues that purpose-driven motivation, or the feeling of doing something meaningful, is a more powerful motivator. He claims that having a sense of purpose and meaningful work is essential for life satisfaction, engagement, and motivation. With much of his research focused on work environments, Pink suggests that organizations can foster a sense of purpose in their employees by creating a clear and compelling mission.

Your family is an organization of sorts. You, an individual, are an organization of thoughts, beliefs, wants, and desires. You are an organization of talents and ideas. Concerning your relationship with your wealth, you and your family need an exciting and purposeful mission to achieve your potential. Likewise, your wealth needs meaning to do all that it can do.

Saving X dollars into an account is not the first step. Neither is investing in ABC mutual fund or implementing such-and-such specific tax strategy. The first step is to find someone who will ask you the questions posed in this book. The first step is to find someone who gives you the tools, wisdom, and guidance to think as big as possible.

In reading this book, you've already taken the first step. Now it's time to keep going.

We've looked at all the reasons you've been hesitating, and we've explored why they aren't valid — why they're actually holding you back from doing something amazing.

We've explored your values and what you want to see happen in the world.

We've looked at what you could do — if you gave yourself permission — and how it could positively affect so many people. By now, you've already been thinking about how that will look, and I'm betting you feel a little excited by that vision, too.

It's up to you. Are you ready to take the next step into a new world you haven't even imagined could exist? Isn't it time to find out what it really looks like?

If you answered yes, then all you have to do is pick up the phone or start an email. Whether that's with me or with another advisor you feel confident about, I wish you the best of luck. And I would love to hear about the journey.

As you begin, keep this thought in mind:

During my first day of training in jiu-jitsu, my heart was racing, and my stomach was churning with nerves when I walked into the gym. The anxiety only worsened once the training started. My sparring partners were black belts — incredibly fit men and women with decades of experience in the art. I was overwhelmed. Using all my strength, athleticism, grit, and determination, I fought back, yet still was as helpless as a small child. My body bent to their will. At the end of the training session, after being utterly humiliated, I picked my white belt off the mat — the attire worn by beginners — and tied it around my waist. With sweat profusely dripping off my reddened cheeks, I muttered, "I didn't realize it would be this hard."

Calvin, a man whose six-pack had a six-pack, heard my negative self-talk and placed his hand on my shoulder. "Remember, man," he said with a grin of understanding, "a black belt is just a white belt who never quit."

There is nothing more noble and brave — nothing more important — than to dare to think big with your money. Dare to think beyond the minutia of investment returns. Dare to think beyond what is in front of you now. Dare yourself to think of the most important thing you could do with your resources and go do that.

I, along with the rest of the world, can't wait to see what you accomplish.

JOSHUA 1:9

How to *Work with Me*

The first step in the journey of transforming wealth to significance is to meet and find the right person to be alongside you on your journey. After reading this, I hope you feel that person is me.

If so, we can set a time to work together for approximately ninety minutes. During that time, we focus our efforts on our Five D Process. In the Discovery and Diagnosis phase, we aim to set you up for success in the Decision Lab.

By the end of our meeting, we will have accomplished two things: One, we'll know if we are the right team to work for you. Two, you will know if you want us to be your team.

After that meeting, we will have identified at least three important opportunity areas for you to work on. If you choose to hire our team beyond that meeting, we can move into the Decision Lab and begin to transform wealth to significance with you.

If not, after going through the process, you'll still be set up for success in the advisory relationship you feel best fits you.

About the *Author*

Sanger Smith is a private wealth advisor and founder of a boutique wealth management firm, Decidedly Wealth Management, in Fort Worth, Texas. The firm specializes in working with family business owner/operator clients to plan for the second phase of their business and their lives. Before Decidedly, Sanger was the managing partner of a large private wealth firm with over $1 billion in assets under advisement, founded by his father.

A graduate of Texas A&M University, Sanger was a member of the Corps of Cadets and studied financial planning.

Sanger has worked to receive several professional designations, including Certified Exit Planning Advisor™ (CEPA™) from the Exit Planning Institute, Behavioral Financial Advisor™ (BFA™) from think2perform, and Accredited Portfolio Management Advisor® (APMA®) from the College for Financial Planning.

When he's not empowering families to make great financial decisions so they may transform wealth to significance, Sanger

---

spends his time training in Brazilian jiu-jitsu, writing eclectic poetry that no one will read, dancing violently to R&B music in his kitchen, volunteering to help young entrepreneurs in Fort Worth, and hosting the "Decidedly" podcast, in which he and his father, Shawn, talk to academics, entrepreneurs, and athletes about how to defeat bad decision-making.

You can reach Sanger at:

✉ sanger@decidedlywealth.com

🌐 www.decidedlywealth.com

📷 @decidedlypodcast

in www.linkedin.com/in/sanger-d-smith-b1690647

Endnotes

1   Sheena S. Iyengar and Mark R. Lepper, "When
    Choice Is Demotivating: Can One Desire Too Much
    of a Good Thing?" *Journal of Personality and Social
    Psychology*, 76, no. 6 (December 2000): 995-1006,
    doi:10.1037//0022-3514.79.6.995

2   John Gantz and David Reinsel, "The Digital Universe
    in 2020: Big Data, Bigger Digital Shadows, and Biggest
    Growth in the Far East," IDC View, December 2012,
    https://assets.ey.com/content/dam/ey-sites/ey-com/en_gl/
    topics/digital/idc-the-digital-universe-in-2020.pdf.

3   U.S. Bureau of Labor Statistics, *Occupational Outlook
    Handbook: Personal Financial Advisors*, (2021 data), modified
    September 8, 2022, https://www.bls.gov/ooh/business-and-
    financial/personal-financial-advisors.htm.

4   Doug Lennick, "The Alignment Model: A Tool for
    Developing Personal and Organizational Excellence,"
    *Journal of Business and Leadership: Research, Practice, and
    Teaching*, 1, no. 1 (2005): 1–12.

5   Jordan Peterson, "Don't Underestimate the Hole Your Absence Would Leave," YouTube video, 0:35, posted February 7, 2023, https://youtu.be/9gMHokXwaN4.

6   The Vanguard Group, "Putting a Value on Your Value: Quantifying Advisor's Alpha," August 12, 2022, https://advisors.vanguard.com/insights/article/IWE_ResPuttingAValueOnValue.

7   Washington Coalition of Sexual Assault Programs, "The Neurobiology of Reactions to Stress," October 2016, https://www.wcsap.org/resources/publications/tips-guides/youth-advocacy-therapy-tips/neurobiology-reactions-stress.

8   Theodore M. Brown and Elizabeth Fee, "Walter Bradford Cannon: Pioneer Physiologist of Human Emotions," *American Journal of Public Health* 92, no. 10 (2002): 1594–1595, https://www.ncbi.nlm.nih.gov/pmc/articles/PMC1447286/.

9   Rosalind K Humphreys and Graeme D Ruxton, "A Review of Thanatosis (Death Feigning) as an Anti-predator Behaviour," *Behavioral Ecology and Sociobiology,* 72, no. 2 (2018): 22, doi:10.1007/s00265-017-2436-8.

10 Norman B. Schmidt, J. Anthony Richey, Michael J. Zvolensky, and Jon K. Maner, "Exploring Human Freeze Responses to a Threat Stressor," *Journal of Behavior Therapy and Experimental Psychiatry* 39, no. 3 (2008): 292-304, doi:10.1016/j.jbtep.2007.08.002.

11 Kirsten Weir, "Feel Like a Fraud?" *gradPSYCH Magazine,* American Psychological Association, November 2013 (archived page), accessed February 28, 2023, https://www.apa.org/gradpsych/2013/11/fraud.

12 Jim Holt, "Time bandits: What Were Einstein and Gödel Talking About?" *New Yorker,* February 20, 2005, www.newyorker.com/magazine/2005/02/28/time-bandits-2

13 Joe Guy, "Waiting. Listening," personal papers, 1986.

14 *Harvard Business Review*, "How to Make Use of Your Anxiety for Positive Results," https://hbr.org/2013/11/how-to-make-use-of-your-anxiety-for-positive-results#:~:text=Research%20participants%20who%20were%20asked,Brooks%20of%20Harvard%20Business%20School.

15 Simon Sinek, *Start with Why: How Great Leaders Inspire Everyone to Take Action* (Penguin Publishing Group, 2011).

16 Brené Brown, *Daring Greatly* (Avery, 2012).

17 Saul Mcleod, "Maslow's Hierarchy of Needs Theory," Simply Psychology, updated March 10, 2023, https://simply-psychology.org/maslow.html.

18 Timothy Ferris, *The 4-Hour Workweek: Escape 9-5, Live Anywhere, and Join the New Rich* (Harmony, 2009).

19 James Clear, *Atomic Habits* (Avery, 2018).

20 John Paull II, "Apostolic Journey to the United States of America: Eucharistic Celebration in Oriole Park at Camden Yards," Baltimore, October 8, 1995, https://www.vatican.va/content/john-paul-ii/en/homilies/1995/documents/hf_jp-ii_hom_19951008_baltimore.html.

21 Victor Frankl, *Man's Search for Meaning* (Beacon Press, 2006).

22 Epictetus, *The Enchiridion*, translated by Elizabeth Carter. Internet Classics Archive, edited by Daniel C. Stevenson, Massachusetts Institute of Technology, 2009, https://classics.mit.edu/Epictetus/epicench.html.

Made in the USA
Middletown, DE
26 May 2023

30866878R00080